LEAD AGAIN

LEAD AGAIN

A Modern Guide to Resilience

NOEL BAGWELL

Author

Counsel & Clarity Publishing™

CONTENTS

Noel R. Bagwell, III
Counsel & Clarity Publishing™
Clarksville, TN, United States
https://counselandclarity.com/
contact@counselandclarity.com

Cover Image by Noel Bagwell.

Special thanks to everyone who made this book possible.

ISBN: 979-8-218-34335-4 (print)

EISBN: 979-8-218-34336-1 (.epub)

Printed in the U.S.

1st Edition. First Printing, 2024.

*This book is dedicated to my son, Liam,
and the love of my life, Devon. I love you
both with all my heart, and I always will.*

ACKNOWLEDGMENTS

THE AUTHOR GRATEFULLY EXTENDS SPECIAL THANKS TO...

... the following people and their contributions to my life, in the absence of which you would not be reading this book. Therefore, I want to sincerely and specifically thank each of these special individuals:

- Henrietta Bagwell, J. Bradley Stephens, Ryan T. Yamada, Fr. Dan Steiner, Mandi Zielinski (Ross), Fr. Benjamin Butler, Dr. Robert Berberich, Reese & Susie Bagwell, Dr. William & Shirley Perrine, David & Carolyn Lacey, Joanne Waikel, Carl & Ann Marie Kahle, Kevin F. Raymond, Barry Pulley, Walter & Angela Jones, Lonny Baggett, Dr. Tim Winters, Dr. Mark Michael, Prof. Tom Stone, and Prof. Jill Evans;

- Matt Corlett, for the many hours of guidance, counseling, and training for which I owe a debt of gratitude that could never be repaid; and

- Katrina Elkins ("Katrina Starr"), for facilitating healing and making connections that have made an enormous difference in my life.

ADDITIONALLY, TO ALL THOSE MENTIONED BY NAME OR CITED IN THIS BOOK:

Thank you for being part of my story, part of the lessons I've learned, part of my life, whether directly or indirectly. I'm grateful to know you, to have learned from you, and count you among my friends, colleagues, or teachers.

CHAPTER 1

Your Guide Through "Lead Again"

How to Engage with This Book

In our world, the only constant is change. This book, *Lead Again*, is meant to be something of a compass through the shifting and sometimes rapidly evolving landscape of 21st Century leadership. In these pages, I don't just write about the surface-level mechanics of leadership. Instead, I want readers to use this work as a starting place to delve deep into the art and science of rising from the ashes of adversity in the contexts both of self-leadership and leadership more generally.

Within these chapters, elements of my own story appear where instructive, serving as a testament to the power of resilience and adaptability in the face of adversity. Sometimes, healing in public inspires and encourages those who are healing in private. I invite you to connect compassionately with my journey, shared vulnerably to illuminate the path of recovery from setbacks for your benefit.

Building on the foundation of compassion, we delve into the interplay between resilience and adaptability—key traits that transform leadership from a role into a journey. I am committed to promoting the balance of rational compassion, activated by discernment. This book demystifies how resilience fuels adaptability, forming the cornerstone of impactful leadership. I have sought to open the kimono on this topic by sharing the wisdom I've learned--both directly, through personal experience, and from studying others.

As you explore this book, I hope you'll seek a nuanced understanding of leadership as a multifaceted endeavor. I want readers to recognize that the true essence of leadership lies not in the loud proclamations of success but in the groundbreaking insights that surface in quiet moments of reflection and recovery following setbacks. You'll find that, in these pages, leadership is not portrayed as a linear ascent up, for example, the corporate ladder. Rather, imagine leadership as undulating waves: each crest symbolizes our triumphs, while every trough represents challenges, offering lessons in adaptability and growth, all of which holistically teach us about resilience.

For instance, the book dives deep into the disciplined pursuit of prioritization, illustrating through real-world examples how focusing on what truly matters can elevate leadership effectiveness. That's a theme that emerges more than once, because I believe great leaders make a powerful effort to focus on what truly matters, cut through the noise of daily life, and engage in the deep work of collaboration toward shared goals.

Additionally, *Lead Again* offers several meditations on the psychological and spiritual resilience necessary for effective leadership. I hope you'll come to appreciate the importance of mindfulness, of being fully present in the moment, and of embracing the inherent uncertainties of leading with the calm confidence that comes from faith. If you engage with these lessons, you will nurture the soil of your mind and cultivate a mindset that sees challenges not as insurmountable obstacles but as stepping stones to greater heights.

This book challenges you to look beyond the façade of traditional leadership, which tends to focus primarily on getting results and material success, and to embrace a more holistic approach, one that values self-awareness and personal growth as key components of professional success.

Deeply engaging with *Lead Again* means embracing leadership not as an end state to be obtained, but as a process – one marked by continuous learning, self-discovery, and the courage to face one's fears head-on. It means embracing self-leadership as the first principle of all leadership.

As you turn these pages, ask yourself: What leadership challenge am I ready to face with resilience and adaptability? Embrace this journey not just as a reader but as an emerging leader, ready to transform every setback into a stepping stone for a greater comeback. There is a better leader within you, waiting to rise from the ashes of your last (or next) setback.

As you explore this book, let me not just tell you how to lead but show you how to cultivate the self-leadership that will bloom into an empowering resilience that empowers you to face the world with renewed strength and clarity.

CHAPTER 2

Igniting the Spark of Leadership

An Introduction to Leadership and Resilience

I didn't write this book to merely motivate; rather, I wrote it to guide the reader to truths that transcend the ordinary leadership narrative. I want readers to use it as a practical tool--a compass for navigating the unpredictable seas of leadership in the face of adversity.

I don't want to convey the message, "Hang in there! It'll get better," because I don't believe that. As Joan Rivers insightfully noted, "It doesn't get better; you get better." These pages are a chronicle of that transformation. Maybe, through your transformation as a leader some things will get better. Maybe they won't. In any event, I want you to know that you can rise above circumstances, environment, and even the powerful storms of emotion they send your way.

In these pages, I invite you to walk with me, step by step, through the valleys and peaks of personal and professional challenges. I can speak to the heights and depths of such experiences, because I've experienced them first hand.

In later chapters, I'll relate how I've lived through many losses, including a family home, once a symbol of success and stability; love and the promise of acceptance, approval, and affection; and even business opportunities. I've felt the sting of loss, tasted the bitter of wine of failure, and flinched at the sound of doors slamming closed on business ventures. I have loved and lost, and sincerely questioned whether Alfred, Lord Tennyson may have been wrong. The anecdotes I share are not merely to illustrate points; often, they are chapters from my life, each a lesson in resilience. Often, they're chapters from my life, each one a lesson in resilience, a valuable treasure I learned in my recovery from one loss or another.

For over a decade as a business lawyer and advisor, I've been a beacon for others weathering their storms. Along with my own personal life lessons, the wisdom I've gained from advising others and from studying resilient leadership has been distilled into actionable insights.

At the end of each chapter, I include Key Takeaways and Action Items, because the heart of this book is eminently practical, because I want each reader to know that their own struggles, while unique, are of a certain kind--the human kind. There is commonality between my loss and yours, in spite of the unique quality of our experiences. And because I've been through the kind of thing you may have experienced--the kind of loss, suffering, or grief, I have a desire to fortify your leadership, to help you weather times of crisis, and emerge stronger on the other end. The lessons in this book were forged in the furnace of suffering, and, therefore, are designed to resonate with your journey, no matter what you've lost, what you're mourning, or what pain is driving you.

Part One: The Foundations of Resilience

In the first part of *Lead Again*, "The Foundations of Resilience," I present what I believe are the essentials of resilience. I wrote these lessons to empower the reader who may be struggling just to stand firm to dancing in the rain of challenges.

So, in this part, I present chapters on the motivation for leadership, the fortitude of will, the rebirth of trust, and the art of self-respect. I also present a challenge to misconceptions about boundaries, discussing how to properly deploy and maintain healthy boundaries without erecting dangerous barriers to personal growth, interpersonal dialogue, forgiveness, and reconciliation.

This part of *Lead Again* also will guide you through the process of understanding how you reinvent yourself, helping you cultivate greater virtue, and building traits others look for in a leader. At the end of Part One, you'll find chapters on dealing with disruption, restoring trust in yourself, and repairing your relationships with others in an authentic way.

Part Two: Navigating the Storm

The second part, "Navigating the Storm," all about the practice of leadership as a discipline. These chapters are about finding the eye of the storm, centering yourself, and learning to thrive in dynamic and complex leadership environments.

One chapter outlines how to assemble a leadership toolkit. There are several chapters devoted to various necessary aspects of the discipline that will allow you to maintain calm, even when things are chaotic. These include mindfulness practices that offer clarity, essentialism strategies that focus your energy, the wholehearted embrace of constructive feedback as a gift, and more.

Together, we'll also explore topics such as the importance of physical and spiritual health, the power of a united team, and the mastery of time, how to make the most of your meetings, among others - each element a vital cog in the machinery of successful leadership.

This part of *Lead Again* is not just a feel-good romp through tired clichés and catchy slogans. Rather, it's a practical guide to both the principles and the practices of the discipline of leadership. Please understand, this makes some of the material in this book difficult to accept. Whenever you find resistance within yourself as you read this book, though, remember, that's where growth happens. Just like lifting weights at the gym, "no pain, no gain;" it's be overcoming resistance in a healthy, constructive way that we get stronger.

Your Ally in Leadership Recovery

Through this book, I hope you come to see me as an ally, a mentor, and a friend on the path to rediscovering your leadership prowess. I may not know you, but I care about you, anyway. I often pray for the readers of this book, as a group. My sincerest hope is that this book will help you.

Whether you're nursing personal wounds, steering through professional turbulence, or both, *Lead Again* is meant to offer wisdom, guidance, and practical tools necessary for healing, growth, and reemergence as a leader--first one who masters self-leadership and then as one who can effectively lead others.

As you turn each page, I would love for you to feel the empowerment seep through the words, although it may take more than one attempt to get there. I hope you'll make an effort, as you go, to hold in your mind a vision of the leader you need to become--resilient, confident, and trustworthy. The exercise of working your way through this book, I hope, will not be merely reading, but committing to a transformative odyssey through which you emerge as a better leader.

So, let's begin. Consider each step you take in these pages to be a step forward in your leadership comeback. Turn the page, and let's embark on this journey together, towards a horizon of resilience and renewed leadership. Ignite the spark, light the torches, and lets head out.

PART ONE

*THE FOUNDATIONS OF
RESILIENCE*

CHAPTER 3

The Need to Lead

Delving into Our Motivations

Understanding your drive to lead is a vital first step in the journey to restore your capacity to lead. Before doing anything else, ask yourself this difficult question: "Why do I need to lead, *now*?" It's important to be honest, and self-aware when surfacing the answer.

Notice, too, that the answer to the question may need to be different from the question, *"In the past*, why have I felt the need to lead?" Part of any setbacks you may have experienced as a leader could derive from poor motivations to lead and their consequences. Thus, discovering new motivations may be essential for the progress you seek in your leadership journey.

Your answer to, "Why do I need to lead, *now*," will lay the groundwork for our leadership approach, and engaging a coach or mentor for deeper insight is often beneficial.[1] The insight you'll gain from answering this question well not only guides your strategic decisions but also shapes how you inspire and connect with your team.

Motivation is central to leadership. Without a strong connection to our leadership motivations, our energy and endurance may falter. However, sometimes the answer to "Why do I need to lead?" is simply, "I don't need to." Some assume leadership roles due to circumstances or opportunities, not from a true passion or need to lead.

In such cases, leadership might be more of a duty than a genuine desire. If that's you, it's okay to step back. Remember the saying, "Lead, follow, or get out of the way." Without passion and internal motivation, it's best to find your passion, follow someone who has it, or step aside from leadership.

Classic Leadership Motives

Now, let's explore some classic motivations to lead. As you read the insights and anecdotes in this section, which shed light on the four principal leadership motives, try to think of any other motives you have had for leading that aren't discussed, here.

With respect to any such motivations, ask yourself, "Are my motives self-focused or altruistic," Are they based on recognition or helping others or existential fulfillment?

Most people want to be seen as team players, as altruistic, as kind and helpful members of our community. Motivation is a complex thing, though--not always simple or clearcut. It may be the case that you have multiple motivations. Some may be more noble than others.

As you contemplate your motivation for leading, be honest with yourself. If you're not, you're only sabotaging your own efforts to improve your capacity for good leadership.

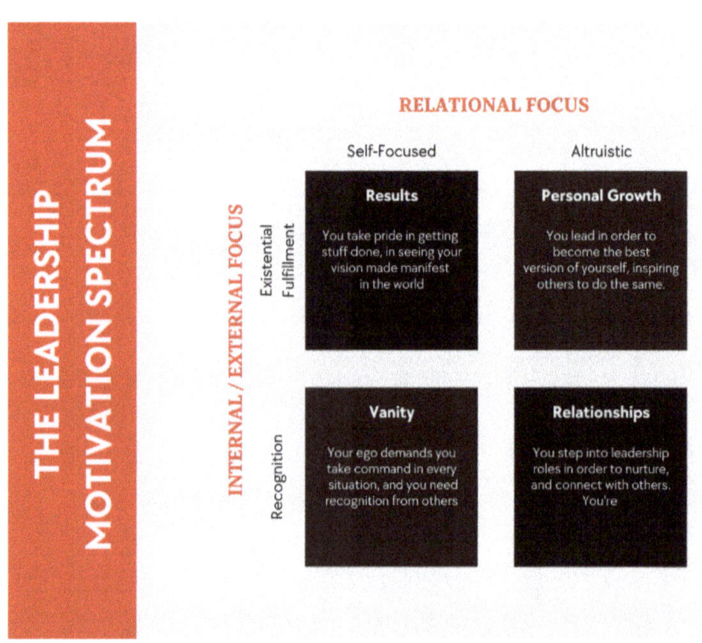

The Leadership Motivation Spectrum

Vanity

Growing up, the frequent predictions of 'You're going to be President someday' filled my younger self with pride. After cultivating emotional maturity and self-awareness, I came to recognize the hidden edge of these praises—they subtly groomed me for a leadership style rooted in vanity, one that I would ultimately strive to transcend.

When we internalize the expectations of others, we can develop a craving for personal accomplishment and acclaim. For some, this desire becomes tied to their self-worth, and when their leadership capacity is impaired, they can feel devastated.

However, vanity can also be an effective motivator if it drives us to excel and bring our organization to the forefront.

Beware, though, vanity can turn leaders into controlling figures. There is always a risk of ego-driven leaders becoming controlling and domineering, making them less effective and more insufferable in the long run.

Relationships

Many people are motivated to lead by the need to be needed or respected. I experienced this shift in my teens and early twenties. At this time in my life, whenever I was given an opportunity to lead, my aim tended to be to connect, participate, and help others with my skills.

For example, on a mission trip to Panama at 17, I earned the lead role in our street drama group. I used my excellent communication skills to build strong relationships and improve our group's morale and effectiveness, providing encouragement and guidance to my teammates.

I loved being the person others would come to for advice, because I felt like I really was helping them, participating in their lives, and actually connecting with them at a human level.

There is an art to giving and receiving advice. Leaders who are motivated by their interpersonal relationships—often driven by an insatiable craving for connection—excel at the art of giving (and receiving) advice.

Skilled advising is not just about the content of the advice, but also about how it is given. It is a creative and collaborative process that requires an ongoing conversation to better understand problems and find solutions. It is not a one-time transaction, but rather a continuous effort to improve understanding and find promising paths forward.

Leaders with this motivation can be amazing managers and motivators. Sometimes, however, they can struggle with making difficult choices between what they see as beneficial for their concrete, interpersonal relationships and the needs of a larger, more abstract organization, such as a company or community.

Results

Another potent motivation that fuels many leaders is the pursuit of results. Individuals propelled by this driving force are primarily concerned with getting things done, accomplishing objectives, and realizing the fruits of their efforts. They're usually energetic, action-oriented, and thrive in an environment where performance is measurable and, more importantly, visible.

Results-oriented leaders tend to be self-motivated, with a mindset keenly focused on achieving their predetermined goals. They tend to be resilient, willing to tackle challenges head-on, and are not easily discouraged by obstacles or setbacks. They display a high level of commitment, investing time, effort, and resources to realize their objectives.

My own journey into results-oriented leadership really came into its fullness when I started my law practice. I was motivated by the idea of building a successful venture, making a tangible impact in my field, and achieving recognition for my work. This was a time of great energy and enthusiasm, as the prospect of manifesting my vision for how smaller law firms could better serve small-to-medium businesses propelled me forward.

The same results-focused drive was carried into a couple of subsequent entrepreneurial endeavors. However, these initial ventures proved challenging. I launched two start-ups with my wife, Devon, both of which did not succeed as I had hoped. The first start-up faltered due to a lack of genuine buy-in from Devon, who simply didn't have the interest that I hoped she would. The second venture failed because of discordant interests within the team of partners that had come together around my idea for the business. There is an intricate relationship between shared vision and results, and I learned from that experience that each key person's expectations need to be fully explored and clearly articulated before moving forward in a new venture.

Looking back, I can see that being solely results-oriented, while having its merits, also blinded me to other necessary considerations. Tunnel vision can cost you a lot! Striving for success is important, but one must also remember to balance this drive with other vital aspects of leadership such as building meaningful relationships, gaining genuine buy-in from your team, and aligning everyone's interests towards a common goal.

While it's important to push toward goals, results-driven leaders must understand the essential and equal importance of ensuring their goals are shared by all the key people involved in an endeavor. After all, achieving lasting results is a team effort, and you can't drag others to your dreams. Rather, the ability to inspire, engage, and support others in the pursuit of shared objectives is the mark of a truly effective leader.

The path of leadership is complex and full of lessons like these. My journey made me realize that being a results-oriented leader also meant growing and adapting, knowing when to persist and when to adjust course. It's about the flexibility to learn from failures and the humility to recognize and address any shortfalls in one's approach to leadership.

A results-driven motivation can be a powerful force in leadership. As with any leadership motivation, however, it needs to be balanced with rational compassion, collaboration, and a clear, shared vision. True leadership success lies not just in the attainment of goals, but also in the journey and growth experienced along the way.

Personal Growth

Personal growth serves as a profound motivation for many leaders. Leaders motivated by personal growth focus on being the best they can be. They're driven by continual improvement, a genuine love of wisdom, and a desire to reach their full potential. This motivation can infuse leadership with a sense of purpose and authenticity.

For me, the journey towards personal growth was ignited by adversity. A significant turning point came after I suffered two nearly simultaneous, life-altering tragedies – the loss of my beloved grandmother and the abrupt dissolution of my fifteen-year marriage. The emotional devastation and financial hardship I faced were immense, and I was presented with two stark options: crumble under the weight of the losses or choose to grow from them. I chose growth.

This choice meant diving headfirst into a journey of self-improvement. It involved sharpening my self-awareness, reassessing my behaviors, challenging my belief systems, and deepening my faith. The quest for personal growth became more than a goal; it became a survival tactic, a beacon that guided me through my darkest moments, an evolution that transformed me into a man reborn.

Over time, this pursuit transformed from a survival tactic into a conscious and intentional motivation. It became a tool for leading others through their hardships, helping them navigate personal and professional setbacks, and fostering their healing. It gave me the strength to lead with renewed purpose and a deep-seated authenticity.

Personal growth has taught me that leadership can be about evolving both individually and together with others who are on a similar path. This kind of evolution transforms pain into power, extracts feedback from failures, and uses such lessons to empower oneself and others. Truly, it is our most painful experiences that often shape us into the leaders we are meant to be. The pursuit of personal growth has allowed me to emerge from adversity stronger and better equipped to lead and support others. If you need evidence that from the ashes of hardship, a resilient leader can arise, here I am.

"Pros and Cons" of Leadership Motives

The benefits and downsides of each motive relate to whether our drive to lead is self-focused or altruistic. Leaders who, at least, appear to be leading for the good of others gain more trust. Indeed, the best leaders are those who lead reluctantly, seeing leadership as guiding others toward shared goals, rather than wielding power.[2]

Consider the example of George Washington, a paradigm of reluctant leadership. His actions and words reflected a sense of duty and selflessness that made him a beloved and respected figure.[3] As the American Revolution came to a successful conclusion, Washington's leadership and military prowess were highly praised. Yet, when the opportunity arose for him to seize more power, he instead chose to relinquish it and retire to his plantation at Mount Vernon, emphasizing his wish for a peaceful private life after eight long years of war.

In 1787, when the Constitutional Convention concluded with a newly minted framework for a stronger federal government, Washington was the unanimous choice to become the first President of the nascent United States of America. He expressed his reluctance to take on this role in a letter to Alexander Hamilton, asking, "Have I not done enough for my country?" His question echoed his genuine desire for respite and showed his lack of ambition for personal power.[Id.]

Washington's reluctant acceptance of the presidency embodied his view of leadership as a duty, not a quest for authority. He saw himself as a servant of the American people, ensuring the survival and growth of the young nation. His leadership style, grounded in humility and a deep sense of civic responsibility, resonates with our understanding of effective leadership. Indeed, leadership is not about wielding power but about guiding others towards shared goals.

"Leadership is not about wielding power, but about guiding others towards shared goals."

What is your grand vision and does your leadership primarily benefit you or others? In answering this question, be honest and authentic about your motivations. Self-deception will hurt you and those who follow you.

Whatever your motives, whether self-centered or altruistic, vanity-driven or focused on others, leadership can have meaningful social benefits. It's crucial to be aware of your motives and align them with your core beliefs and values. A coach or mentor can provide valuable support in this process.[4]

Understanding our motivations for leading is vital for our leadership journey. By exploring different motives and being honest about our own, we can ensure that our leadership is in line with our values and goals, benefiting both ourselves and others.

Key Takeaways

- Understanding your motivations for leadership is crucial for your leadership journey.
- Different motives for leadership include vanity, relationships, results, and personal growth, each with its own pros and cons.
- Authenticity and alignment with your core beliefs and values are key in effective leadership.
- Seeking support from a coach or mentor can be beneficial in understanding and navigating your leadership motivations.

Action Items

- Reflect on your own motivations for leadership. Are they rooted in vanity, relationships, results, personal growth, or a combination of these?
- Consider the "pros" and "cons" of your primary leadership motive. How does it impact your leadership style and effectiveness?
- Assess the alignment between your leadership motivations and your core beliefs and values. If there's a misalignment, what steps can you take to address it?
- If you're finding it challenging to understand or navigate your leadership motivations, consider seeking support from a coach or mentor.

CHAPTER 4

The Will to Lead

What Tae Kwon Do Taught Me About How to Be a Kick-Ass Leader

Baek-jeol-bul-gul or "Indomitable Spirit" is a core principle of Tae Kwon Do. As a teenage student of the Korean martial art, I learned that success may not come on the first attempt, whether it be breaking a board with a punch or breaking a bad habit. Possessing an indomitable spirit is absolutely essential for a resilient leader.

Indomitable means being "unconquerable" and having the courage and self-confidence to persist despite setbacks. It is not the absence of fear, but the determination to act in its presence.

An indomitable spirit is not solely a result of innate resilience or obstinacy, but can be cultivated through the cultivation of virtues such as gratitude, hope, joy, and inner peace.

Focusing on these virtues develops a more indomitable spirit, enhancing courage in adversity. Without doing this sometimes challenging work, eventually you'll get knocked down in life and find yourself without the will to get back up. Merely resolving to never give up is insufficient. You have to cultivate the virtues that generate the grace to sustain your will through any trial, starting with gratitude.

Gratitude

For much of my life, I had a limited understanding of gratitude. I often acted as though I were entitled to life's blessings and never fully appreciated them. I was consumed by a desire to maintain a certain quality of life and constantly pursue advancements.

This changed abruptly when my wife blindsided me with a divorce after 15 years. The emotionally devastating, humbling experience taught me genuine humility and the importance of gratitude. I came to appreciate my close relationships with my son, parents, and closest friends far more deeply.

Before the experience, I had believed in the unbreakable bond of family and marriage, but the loss of my beloved wife made me realize that I did not truly know the hearts and minds of others as I thought I had. The trauma led me to re-evaluate everything, from my deepest beliefs to my past and present perceptions. I was forced to accept that my understanding was far more limited than I had realized.

My experience taught me that gratitude isn't just personal; it's a foundational element of effective leadership, turning challenges into opportunities for growth. This personal journey underscores the transformative power of gratitude in leadership. The trauma, grief, and the psychological and physical toll it took on me, eventually gave way to gratitude and a greater appreciation for life's lessons and simple joys.

Joy

Gratitude leads to joy; appreciating what we have makes feeling joy inevitable. Humbly acknowledging that we have been blessed with more than we deserve, creates a sense of happiness and pleasure.

Joy's contagious nature means it readily spreads to those around us. My son loves robots, especially Transformers robots. Once, I bought him two Transformers that he really loved.

As we were picking up some other items in the store, he shouted to a passing employee, "I got *two Transformers!*"

The man had been walking past us towards the back, clearly thinking about the work he was about to do, but my son's joyful information over-share stopped him in his tracks.

At first, he seemed a little confused, but my son repeated his exclamation, and the man replied, "Two Transformers?! That's awesome! They're really cool, aren't they?"

My son said, "Yeah, they're Soundwave and Road Rocket!"

He just couldn't keep to himself his happiness and pleasure with his new toys.

Just as my son's joy over his Transformers was infectious, so too can a leader's genuine joy energize and motivate their team, creating a positive and productive work environment. In the same way, a leader's enthusiasm and positive outlook can inspire and uplift an entire team.

Similarly, converts to a religion often feel a sense of joy and enlightenment in their newfound faith. This joy compels them to share their beliefs with others and inspires hope for what the future may bring.

Joy is a powerful emotion that brings people together and inspires hope for a better future.

Hope

Hope is the practical expression of optimism. It is the manifestation of faith that, with effort, things can improve. Optimism is about expecting good things, while hope involves taking action to achieve what we desire.

Hope became essential for my indomitable spirit. It taught me that with hope, I could not be defeated and would persevere, even in the face of setbacks. Hope drives us to keep trying and motivates us to never give up.

Fostering hope requires more than just wishing. It involves creating a plan and being proactive, even in the face of obstacles. Hopeful people plan for anticipated challenges, not just expecting things to work out. They remain positive and believe that they will find solutions, even if they encounter difficulties.

Hope is not just wishful thinking, but a proactive approach to life that empowers us to overcome adversity and achieve our goals.

There's a great scene in *Dumb and Dumber (1994)*, in which Jim Carey's character, Lloyd Christmas, is trying to gauge his odds of ending up with Lauren Holly's character, Mary Swanson. The dialogue is classic:

Lloyd Christmas: "I want to ask you a question, straight out, flat out, and I want you to give me the honest answer. What do you think the chances are of a guy like you and a girl like me ending up together?"

Mary Swanson: "Well Lloyd, that's difficult to say. We really don't..."

Lloyd Christmas: "Hit me with it! Just give it to me straight! I came a long way just to see you Mary, just... The least you can do is level with me. What are my chances?"

Mary Swanson: "Not good."
[the background soundtrack music suddenly stops]

Lloyd Christmas: [he gulps, his mouth twitching] "You mean, not good like one out of a hundred?"

Mary Swanson: "I'd say more like one out of a million."

Lloyd Christmas: [long pause while he processes what he's heard] *"So you're telling me there's a chance. YEAH!"*

As leaders, nurturing hope means fostering a culture where every possibility is explored and every team member feels empowered to contribute. This principle of hope is vital in leadership, where cultivating an optimistic, can-do attitude within teams can drive innovation and persistence in the face of challenges. In fact, a degree of uncertainty, especially when the odds are not in one's favor, can even nurture hope. So, appreciate uncertainty, and don't let it freeze you in your tracks.

Hopeful individuals have a positive outlook, focusing on what is working well rather than dwelling on negativity. They also find strength in community, connecting with like-minded individuals who share their hopes and aspirations.

To sustain hope, it is essential to remain grounded in reality and use observation to justify continued efforts. Ignoring evidence in favor or against one's hope can lead to delusion and unrealistic thinking.

Hope requires practical optimism, and when optimism becomes unrealistic, it turns into mere wishful thinking. As in the example of Lloyd, chasing an impossible dream without considering evidence leads to absurdity and failure.

Hope is an essential component of the indomitable spirit and requires a positive outlook, a supportive community, and a practical approach to life. By combining these elements, one can achieve their goals and overcome adversity.

Inner Peace

The second part of this book contains more lessons for cultivating inner peace. So, I will only briefly touch on this topic, here. When it comes to forging an indomitable spirit, inner peace acts as the cooling water that hardens the steel, solidifying resolve.. Joy burns like a fire and hope is the malleable metal, but inner peace is the cooling water that solidifies everything.

St. Paul, the Apostle wrote, in his Epistle to the Church at Philippi:

"Not that I complain of want; for I have learned, in whatever state I am, to be content. I know how to be abased, and I know how to abound; in any and all circumstances I have learned the secret of facing plenty and hunger, abundance and want."[5]

This is inner peace. Inner peace is not ignoring your circumstances. Inner peace is embracing with gratitude your circumstances, whatever they are, trusting that all is as it should be, according to God's will.

A Zen Buddhist kōan presents inner peace this way:

"Before enlightenment: chop wood, carry water.
After enlightenment: chop wood, carry water."

If you're unfamiliar with kōans, they are similar to parables, wise sayings, or stories. There are several ways to read this kōan. Before getting into those, however, I want to say a brief word about "enlightenment."

In Zen Buddhist tradition, "enlightenment" refers to a deep, transformative insight into the nature of reality and self. It represents an awakening to the interconnectedness of all things and the dissolution of the illusion of separateness.

As a devout Catholic, I cannot agree that "enlightenment" necessarily entails the dissolution of the illusion of separateness. While we all have the capacity for interconnectedness, paradoxically, we also are each individuals. This is one of the great spiritual mysteries of human experience.

So, when I contemplate "enlightenment" (for example, when I'm reading Zen literature, which I find fascinating), I tend to consider the unity with God and one another that Christians find in and through the Eucharist, worthily received. This is the source and summit of the Christian faith, and it is a profoundly transcendental experience.

Returning to the kōan, however, one way to read it is that, while nothing appears to have changed, in fact, everything has changed. On a superficial level, the level of action, everything is *status quo*, but, on an existential level, the meaning, value, and purpose given to the actions taken has completely transformed them.

Whether your understanding is Christian or Buddhist, at a practical level, the kōan's meaning is essentially the same (though the transcendental path is markedly different).

We cultivate inner peace when our actions align with who we choose to be. When we intentionally pursue this alignment each action we take begins in a place of deep meaning, purpose, and value. We become fully ourselves when we align our Doing Mind with our Being Mind.

Eckhart Tolle wrote, in *A New Earth: Awakening to Your Life's Purpose*:

"Doing is never enough if you neglect Being. The ego knows nothing of being but believes you will eventually be saved by doing. If you are in the grip of the ego, you believe that by doing more and more you will eventually accumulate enough 'doings' to make yourself feel complete at some point in the future. You won't. You will only lose yourself in doing. The entire civilization is losing itself in doing that is not rooted in Being and thus becomes futile."

Another way to read the "chop wood, carry water" kōan is that all activities are objectively the same, and enlightenment allows us to find liberation and salvation from learned negative associations we have attached to various activities.

"Before Enlightenment ... You chop wood and carry water, but secretly wish to get out of it all. ... In a way, you are a victim, a slave — the wood chops you and the water carries you, and there is no way to escape ... After Enlightenment, you are in harmony with the universe ... so you see that there is nothing more important than chopping wood and carrying water. All activities are equalized, there is no preference, no discrimination. Because there is no 'you', no ego, no personality, no being, no separate individuality — there is no conflict. No need to escape...because you have mastered your mind, you are not chopped by the wood and carried by the water anymore. You can flip your perspective at will. It is your choice to chop wood and carry water ..."[6]

Enlightenment allows us, at will, to assign to any activity whatever value we choose. Even tasks as mundane as chopping wood or carrying water can become spiritually enriching. For leaders, achieving inner peace translates into a calm, composed presence that steadies the team, even during turbulent times. Therefore, a leader's inner peace is not just a personal sanctuary; it's a source of strength and stability that can guide an entire organization through adversity.

A third way to read the "chop wood, carry water" kōan is a bit more axiomatic: life goes on. I dislike this reading, because it devalues enlightenment, and implicitly presupposes that one can obtain inner peace without achieving enlightenment—a notion I regard with extreme skepticism.

Nevertheless, there is something to be said about inner peace, here. If one truly has found inner peace, even the experience of achieving enlightenment (or failing to have done so) does not trouble our hearts or minds to a great degree.

One may say, "Before enlightenment: life. After enlightenment: life. Life goes on, whether or not one has learned to live in harmony with it." This strikes me as particularly nihilistic or detached to an unhealthy degree from life; so, I consider it disruptive to inner peace, even if one could argue that there is a certain stillness to be experienced in the heat death of the universe. While I dislike this interpretation, it's worth noting, because it's one that many people have embraced.

"Doing is never enough if you neglect Being."
-- ECKHART TOLLE

For the leader, I believe, inner peace should be understood the way St. Paul describes it, the first way the "chop wood, carry water" kōan has been interpreted, above. This is the practice I believe leaders should pursue.

What one does ought to be rooted in who he is, his very being, his character, his values, and his authentic worldview. When this happens, each of one's actions become valuable, acquire meaningful purpose, and nurture his inner peace.

Reflect on your own virtues and how they contribute to your leadership style. This alignment between action and authentic self is what defines true leadership. Now, I encourage you to reflect on how your virtues shape your approach to leading others.

KEY TAKEAWAYS

- The "Indomitable Spirit" is a core principle of leadership, embodying courage and persistence in the face of adversity.
- Cultivating virtues such as gratitude, joy, hope, and inner peace can help develop an indomitable spirit.
- Authenticity and alignment with your core beliefs and values are key in effective leadership.
- Inner peace in leadership is achieved when one's actions are rooted in their being, character, values, and authentic worldview.

ACTION ITEMS

- Reflect on your own virtues and how they contribute to your leadership style. Are you cultivating gratitude, joy, hope, and inner peace?
- Consider how you can develop an indomitable spirit in your leadership. What steps can you take to embody courage and persistence?
- Assess the alignment between your actions and your being. Are your actions rooted in your character, values, and authentic worldview?
- If you're finding it challenging to achieve inner peace in your leadership, consider seeking support from a coach or mentor.

CHAPTER 5

The Currency to Lead

Why You Can't Lead, Right Now: You're Broke as the Ten Commandments

When I was young, my father passed on wisdom he received from his father that I'll share with you. He said, "Friends are like money in the bank." I've never been entirely comfortable with how transactional that feels, as if people are merely commodities to be used.

I'm certain, however, that's not what my grandfather or father intended. Rather, this aphorism speaks to the *value* of relationships, which ties into the most crucial aspect of leadership: trust.

Observing relationships through a transactional lens, however, does offer unique insights, though it's crucial not to let this be the *only* perspective. When viewed as a marketplace, inter-subjective dynamics spotlight some undeniable truths about trust and leadership.

In leadership, trust is like money in the bank. If you're struggling to lead, it's because, as far as potential followers are concerned, your account, so to speak, is drained of trust. Trust is what you need to create "buy-in" for your ideas, goals, and agenda.

Trust is the most important currency in the 'market' for followers. If you can't lead, it's because you're broke as the Ten Commandments. That is, you are trust-poor – you lack the necessary currency to influence others to take the actions you'd like them to take.

Of course, the next question is: When one has no currency (i.e., trust), how does he go from rags to riches? That's what we'll explore in the remainder of this chapter.

"If you're having trouble leading, you're probably having trouble listening."

There are, at least, six ways a person builds up the currency of trust. There may be more, but these six are tried and true. I should caution you, however, that, just as in business, if something seems too good to be true, it probably is. If, outside these pages, you've been exploring a trust-building approach that seems as tempting as a get-rich-quick scheme, it's probably bogus.

None of these are going to make you trust-rich overnight, but they are reliable means by which to gradually and consistently build trust in your relationships. Without further ado, here they are.

THE ART OF BUILDING TRUST THROUGH RAPPORT

While skills like reading, writing, and speaking can be satisfyingly explored in one's educational journey, he is far less likely to be trained to master the art of establishing rapport and building authentic trust. At the heart of trust-building is rapport, which fosters open communication through a state of harmonious understanding. Mastering the art of establishing and boosting rapport is an essential skill for anyone who wants to build trust and, therefore, for every leader.

Rapport goes beyond surface-level agreement or comprehension, embodying a deeper connection where individuals influence and respond to each other effectively. Rapport is a gateway through which we can intersubjectively transact with one another, establishing and nurturing trust.

A good starting point is to improve how you listen—a skill often overlooked in education. American philosopher Mortimer J. Adler, in his book *How to Speak, How to Listen*, has shed light on a crucial aspect of rapport-building: active engagement or listening.

Adler writes, "The meeting of two minds may consist in their understanding of one another while still in disagreement or it may consist in their coming into agreement as a result of their understanding one another."

Agreement is not required for a meeting of the minds! Active engagement, however, is an indispensable component of rapport, a vital foundation for trust-building.

This is a point that seems lost on many people today. The modern consensus seems to be that if you disagree with someone, you're not listening to them. But that's a false assumption. One can both listen *and* disagree.

It's arrogant to assume that if someone remains unpersuaded by our argument, they weren't listening or didn't understand. Underneath this belief is an assumption either that one's point of view is the only possibly correct perspective or that one has been perfectly persuasive, or both.

Adler shares another important idea about conversations that ties directly to our topic of building trust. He puts it this way:

"All impersonal conversations, whether theoretical or practical in aim, should strive to conclude with a meeting of minds in one or the other form in which that can be achieved. Practical conversations are often unsuccessful because misunderstanding prevents them from reaching a decision. Even with sufficient understanding present, disagreement can block the way to action."

However, I would respectfully add that personal conversations should also aim for a meeting of the minds. To earn the trust of others, we must have a meeting of the minds. Even if we don't persuade our conversation partner, if we demonstrate integrity and charity in our communication, we can still earn their trust by being seen as sincere and well-intentioned. This, at least, positions one to be seen as more likable.

As long as others see us as likable, we will maintain a certain minimum of trust currency with them. If, however, we come across as unlikable or fail to reach a meeting of minds, we lose trust currency with them. This is due to the inverse of a cognitive bias called the "Halo Effect." The Halo Effect occurs when how much we like someone influences our other judgments of them. The inverse can also be powerful: how much we dislike someone can influence our other judgments of them, including our willingness to trust them.

Trust-building in conversations is most effective when both parties reach a mutual understanding and appreciate each other.

RAPPORT AND THE SIX FACETS OF TRUST-BUILDING

Before we delve into the six facets of trust-building, it's essential to understand why each is pivotal. Trust is not monolithic; it's multifaceted, with each aspect contributing uniquely to the foundation of strong, resilient leadership.

These facets work synergistically, much like the ingredients in a recipe, where each is necessary to achieve the desired outcome. By mastering these elements, leaders can establish a robust trust with their teams, paving the way for effective collaboration, innovation, and shared success.

Thus, building trust involves a comprehensive approach that encompasses several key strategies, each vital in its own right and all working together to forge deeper connections. Here are the critical components and how they interconnect to elevate the art of leadership through authentic trust-building:

1. **Authentic Communication**: Involves engaging actively, expressing yourself authentically, and cultivating rapport.

2. **Value Contribution**: Consistently providing valuable insights or assistance to others.

3. **Trustworthy Associations**: Aligning yourself with reliable and respected individuals or groups.

4. **Shared Values**: Finding common values can create stronger bonds and foster trust.

5. **Transparency**: Sharing relevant information and being open about your intentions.

6. **Shared Interests**: Identifying and engaging with common interests can enhance rapport and trust.

PATIENCE: TRUST-BUILDING AS AN ONGOING PROCESS

Patience isn't just a good-to-have in building trust; it's critical. Trust doesn't spring up instantly. Imagine planting a seed and expecting it to bloom right away; that's not how it works, and the same goes for trust. It's built over time, with actions that show you're reliable and communication that's honest.

Think about putting together a puzzle. Each piece you add helps complete the picture, but you can't force pieces where they don't fit, nor can you rush to see the whole image after only a few pieces. In a similar way, building trust is piece by piece—each action or choice that shows your integrity adds up. One act of reliability might not convince someone to trust completely, but as you add more, the evidence of your character becomes undeniable.

So, patience in trust-building means committing to the long haul, knowing that every positive step, every right decision, and every moment of genuine interaction is another piece of the puzzle. It's realizing that trust comes from accumulation, not a single event.

KEY TAKEAWAYS

- Trust is integral to effective leadership.
- Rapport, involving active engagement, is paramount in trust-building.
- Trust can be nurtured through authentic communication, contributing value, aligning with trustworthy individuals or groups, sharing values, providing transparency, and finding shared interests.
- Building trust requires patience and a willingness to adjust your approach.

ACTION ITEMS

- Practice rapport-building in your next three conversations, focusing on active engagement, and then reflect on the experience. After these conversations, reflect on moments where active engagement made a noticeable difference.
- Consider the six facets of trust-building. Identify the ones you are already implementing and those you could work on.
- Evaluate the level of trust in your relationships. If it's low, develop a strategy to rebuild it using the six facets.
- Take a moment to pause and reassess your approach if you've encountered a setback. Re-chart your course with fresh insights.

The Resilient Leader's Path

Balancing Self-Care with Loving Endurance

We all have relationships in our lives that can be challenging, whether it's a friend, family member, or significant other. Even our relationships with certain ideas or ideologies can powerfully affect us. Sometimes, these relationships can be emotionally fraught, causing us to feel hurt, frustrated, or even angry. These relationships, similar to "emotional cacti," promise emotional support but often involve navigating through prickly challenges to reach it.

Think about the classic story from the Bible, the Prodigal Son. The younger son asks his father for his share of the family wealth. He then leaves home, causing his dad a lot of emotional pain. For the father, this is like being pricked by a cactus--not just once but through full-body contact. His dad feels incredibly hurt and upset, but, of course, he still loves his son.

This story really puts into perspective what it's like to handle an "emotional cactus" in our lives. This is the way it is with an emotional cactus - each interaction, a mix of love and pain. Our love, our hope draws us in, hoping for a deep connection, but the sting of rejection, of disregard, of contempt, or of indifference keeps us from the nourishment we seek.

Later, in the parable, when the son comes back, sorry for his actions, his dad's happiness overshadows the earlier pain. Not every story ends so well, though. Sometimes, you find a way to the water inside the cactus. Sometimes, you don't.

It's easy to get stuck in these relationships, especially when fear of change or the unknown prevails. We may hold onto these emotional cacti because we're afraid of being alone or losing a connection to someone who's important to us. We may also believe that the person means well and doesn't intend to hurt us, so we make excuses for their behavior and rationalize their actions.

However, clinging to these emotional cacti can seriously harm our emotional and mental well-being, potentially causing psychological suffering, anxiety, and depression. Navigating the spines of an emotional cactus requires serious commitment and a thoughtful approach.

"Feeling an emotion does not mean 'being in' that emotion."

Ending the Embrace

The first step in handling emotional cacti properly is identifying them. This can include challenging relationships, emotionally disruptive attachments to political views, or any form of longing that leads to suffering.

Secondly, one must practice mindful awareness of the cactus. Observe it, allow it, and accept it for what it is without trying to change it. You might wonder what these prickly traits are protecting the "cactus" from. What does the cactus need? How can I best understand it. Be careful, however, not to fall into psychoanalysis, projection, mind-reading, and the like. Here, instead, practice sympathy for the cactus, instead of applying to it your own judgments as labels.

The third step is to create and enforce an emotional boundary to create distance between ourselves and the source of suffering. The space created should be a minimum effective dose of distance sufficient to give you the ability to be present with the "cactus" without being injured. Regarding this space, it would be a mistake to believe "more is better." Rather, you simply want to create breathing room.

The fourth step is to examine the wound caused by the emotional cactus from a new perspective, now that you have created emotional distance. Why does the way you encounter this "cactus" hurt you? Are their prickly traits dangerous to everyone, or are you especially vulnerable; and, why might that be?

The fifth step is to treat the wound by restoring emotional safety and healing emotional injury. Listen to your mind and body, and respond with mindful and intentional care for yourself. Meditate with your own feelings, inviting them to teach you the lessons they offer. When you are hurt, triggered by a "cactus," your subconscious mind is presenting to your awareness an opportunity to resolve conflict, not only with others but within yourself.

In fact, before you can safely navigate the space around the cactus or develop any strategy for reaching the nourishing waters within it, first, you will need to have resolved the conflicts within yourself by addressing the points where the "cactus" wounds you. This process is like putting on heavy leather gloves or a heavy leather apron. You understand how the cactus hurts you; so, you take precautions. You don't just break all the cactus's spines, because that will damage it. Instead, you simply address your own vulnerabilities.

The boundaries we deploy, here, are not walls. They are not meant to isolate us or perfectly protect us. They allow us to handle others with care for them and for ourselves.

It's especially important to note, here, I would never advocate for cutting down the cactus--removing it from your life. All I'm saying is that you should stay out of range of its spikes, and work out a way to get the nourishment you desire without impaling yourself on the pokey bits--a task that likely will require a great deal of patience and care.

Saving the Scorpion

While, it's important to handle cactus people with care, as they can wound us, sometimes we need to take an intentional and even sacrificially loving approach to people who we know will hurt us.

Rather than avoiding them, sometimes, we need to endure the pain for a greater purpose.

When facing this kind of a challenge, the support of a mentor or coach can be a critical resource in navigating these relationships. They can help us remember to reframe and stay focused on the good we're trying to do, rather than getting drawn into our feelings.

Feeling an emotion does not mean "being in" that emotion. Especially when we expect to face difficult emotions, we ought to make a decent effort to expand our conscious awareness to be larger than any individual feeling, to bring each feeling back into harmony within us, and to avoid becoming or remaining swallowed up by feelings that, in their expression, have grown disproportionately large.

There's a story about a monk and a scorpion that comes to mind when thinking about people who repeatedly hurt us, even when we are trying to help them.

Two monks were washing their bowls in the river when they noticed a scorpion that was drowning.

One monk immediately scooped it up and set it upon the bank. In the process, he was stung.

This scene then played out again when the scorpion fell back in the river, and the monk saved it once more and was stung again.

The other monk asked him, "Friend, why do you continue to save the scorpion when you know it's nature is to sting?"

"Because," the monk replied, "to save it is my nature."

Saving a scorpion is not clinging thoughtlessly to that which causes us suffering, but an intentional, mindful act of sacrificial love based on care and concern for others' needs.

Understanding the distinction between enduring pain for a purpose and unnecessary suffering can help us respond appropriately in different situations.

"Cactus" or "Scorpion"?

As you work to become a stronger leader by enhancing your holistic well-being, you'll encounter both "Cacti" and "Scorpions." Knowing how to identify and respond to each is key to appropriately responding to them.

The Emotional "Cacti"

These are relationships or situations that promise emotional sustenance but come with painful consequences.

Remember that these emotional cacti aren't simply sources of suffering. Often, they are enticing, appearing as a source of emotional nourishment or familiarity. This is especially true in an interpersonal context.

A cactus might be a relationship that provides a sense of validation or an attachment that offers a comforting routine. They could even be beliefs or viewpoints that validate our biases, helping us feel secure and affirmed. However, the truth often lies hidden beneath these appealing aspects - just like a cactus, what seemed nurturing from a distance, up close reveals its prickly thorns. The challenge lies in acknowledging this reality and then deciding how to navigate these complex emotional terrains.

They are characterized by:

- An emotional attachment causing consistent distress.
- A relationship where the pain outweighs the nourishment.
- A situation that drains more energy than it gives.
- A sense of suffering that comes without purpose or growth.

When you identify a "Cactus" in your life, the goal should be to create emotional boundaries, allowing you to disengage from the suffering and focus on self-care and healing.

The "Scorpion"

Unlike a "Cactus," a "Scorpion" situation requires us to willingly endure the pain for a greater purpose. This might mean:

- Staying in a challenging situation for the sake of love, compassion, or duty.
- Accepting short-term suffering for long-term gain.
- Persisting through pain because the end goal aligns with your core values and purpose.

In "Scorpion" situations, remember to maintain mindfulness, grounding yourself in your larger purpose rather than being consumed by and reactive to the immediate pain.

While "Cacti" and "Scorpions" both involve emotional discomfort, the key difference lies in (1) whether the sting or prickle is intentionally directed at you and (2) your response. For "Cacti," the ideal approach, usually, is to establish boundaries and foster self-care. For "Scorpions," the focus is on endurance, growth, and commitment to a purpose beyond immediate comfort. In dealing with both "Cacti" and "Scorpions", what ultimately guides our actions should be a purposeful intent to grow and love mindfully--sometimes more focused on our own needs, sometimes more focused on the needs of others.

Pushing Past Peril with Purpose

The goal of personal growth should not be the avoidance of suffering, but the development of the capacity for living with intentional, mindful, sacrificial love for everyone.

Letting go of a cactus person can be difficult, especially if they have been a source of comfort, familiarity, and validation for a long time. If they are causing suffering without purpose, it's time to face facts and get some distance.

Don't shy away from asking for support from a mentor or coach to get help through the process of developing healthy boundaries and expanding your awareness. Lean on them for emotional support, insight to heal from past hurts, and guidance on how to handle difficult relationships in a healthier way.

Developing the capacity for transcendental love, rather than simply clinging to the comfort of the familiar, is what brings true dignity and respect to our lives as human beings, created in the image of God.

As you authentically embrace genuine self-respect, perhaps for the first time, remember that both "cacti" and "scorpions" are natural parts of our emotional environments. Handle each appropriately: distance yourself from the "cacti" that cause more pain than give nourishment, while embracing the "scorpions" when love and purpose demand it.

In leadership and in life, our purpose is not to avoid discomfort, but to grow in our capacity for intentional, mindful, and sacrificial love. Self-respect blooms when we can navigate these emotional territories with discernment and grace.

KEY TAKEAWAYS

- Emotional cacti are relationships or attachments that offer emotional sustenance but also cause pain and suffering. Identifying, observing, and accepting these is crucial.
- Establishing emotional boundaries can protect our emotional and psychological well-being from emotional cacti.
- Emotional healing, in part, involves self-care practices like mindfulness or self-compassion.
- "Scorpion" situations require endurance and compassion as they involve willingly enduring pain for a greater purpose.
- Mentors or coaches can provide valuable support in navigating challenging emotional terrains.
- Personal growth encompasses developing the capacity for purposeful, considerate, sacrificial love for everyone, and not merely avoiding suffering.

ACTION ITEMS

- Reflect on your relationships and identify any "emotional cacti" in your life. Be specific about why you categorized them as such, considering the balance of emotional nourishment and pain they provide.
- Practice creating emotional boundaries with these relationships or attachments. Consider specific steps such as communicating your feelings to the other party, limiting the time you spend engaging with them, or seeking advice from a mental health professional.
- Explore therapeutic techniques such as mindfulness or self-compassion to promote emotional healing. This could involve activities like guided meditations, journaling your thoughts and feelings, or attending workshops or therapy sessions on these topics.
- Identify any "scorpion" situations in your life and consider ways you can approach them with mindful endurance and compassion. Be specific about your strategy, whether that involves reframing your perspective, seeking support, or practicing acceptance.
- Seek support from a mentor or coach if you're struggling with challenging relationships or emotions. Consider discussing specific issues you're facing and ask for advice on coping mechanisms, perspective shifts, or other strategies.
- Reflect on your personal growth goals. Are they aligned with the goal of developing the capacity for intentional, conscious, benevolent care for everyone? Consider writing these goals down and thinking about specific steps you can take to achieve them.

CHAPTER 7

Leadership Under Fire

Reclaiming Your Professional Standing

A good reputation is a necessary asset for any effective leader. A single misstep can ripple through your professional standing, leaving you scrambling to reclaim the trust and confidence that once felt secure. To help you navigate these challenges, I've created a process called "Reputation Triage" - a system tailored to help you restore your reputation and reclaim the trust of those who matter most.

Like the medical triage process that categorizes patients based on the severity of their injuries, Reputation Triage requires leaders to assess the impact of their words and actions, prioritize tasks and conversations, and leverage outside perspectives.

To illustrate how triage works, generally, let me tell you a brief story. When I was 15, I got hit by a car while riding my mountain bike on a busy road. I ended up in the emergency room with a broken kneecap and asphalt that had to be scraped out of my left shoulder and right knee from where I'd tumbled and skidded across the road.

As rough as I felt like I had it, at the time, there were people in the E.R. who were much worse off. Doctors had to triage, prioritizing my treatment and others' based on the severity of my injuries.

Similarly, much like this, leaders have to evaluate their situation when their reputation suffers a serious blow and take decisive steps towards recovery. You have to address the right issues by order of priority. Your situation dictates the priority. Treating each of the "patients," however, is important.

This system stands on four pillars:

- Accept Responsibility,
- Bring Awareness to the Situation,
- Conscientiously Communicate and Conciliate, and
- Do Not Lie, Blame, or Shame.

By embracing this process, leaders can start to treat their damaged reputation, fortify their leadership skills, enrich their relationships, and improve their personal and professional life. In the following pages, we'll break down each of the pillars of the Reputation Triage system.

Accept Responsibility

In his book, *Radical Responsibility*, Fleet Maull provides profound insights on shifting away from blame and fear-based coping strategies. Embracing ownership for every circumstance, according to Maull, ushers in a life of fearlessness and positions you as a force for good. To make this shift, focus on solutions instead of *dwelling* on problems. Here's how you can achieve this:

- Claim ownership of your circumstances.

- Use reflective language, like "I'm angry," instead of projective language, like "You made me angry."

- Ask empowering questions to propel yourself forward.

- Learn from experiences and modify your approach in the future.

Such actions demonstrate your integrity and accountability, elements that forge trust.

Bring Awareness to the Situation

In *Thinking, Fast and Slow*, Daniel Kahneman underscores the importance of seeking an outside perspective when evaluating a plan or decision. Taking an "outside view" can involve observing similar circumstances, consulting statistical information from similar ventures, or asking a knowledgeable person for their insight. This will help bring greater awareness to your situation and can lead to more informed decision-making.[7]

In *Thinking, Fast and Slow*, Kahneman writes of his work with his research partner, "Amos and I coined the term *planning fallacy* to describe plans and forecasts that are unrealistically close to best-case scenarios[, and] could be improved by consulting the statistics of similar cases."

Gaining an outside perspective might simply mean looking at situations similar to yours, and considering that you're in a situation that's more common than you probably realized before you found yourself in it! Then, observe how other people successfully maneuvered through the situation to a more desirable position relative to their circumstances.

"The renowned Danish planning expert Bent Flyvbjerg, now at Oxford University, offered a forceful summary:

The prevalent tendency to underweight or ignore distributional information is perhaps the major source of error in forecasting. Planners should therefore make every effort to frame the forecasting problem so as to facilitate utilizing all the distributional information that is available.

This may be considered the single most important piece of advice regarding how to increase accuracy in forecasting through improved methods. Using such distributional information from other ventures similar to that being forecasted is called taking an 'outside view' and is the cure to the planning fallacy. The treatment for the planning fallacy has now acquired a technical name, reference class forecasting, and Flyvbjerg has applied it to transportation projects in several countries. The outside view is implemented by using a large database, which provides information on both plans and outcomes for hundreds of projects all over the world, and can be used to provide statistical information about the likely overruns of cost and time, and about the likely underperformance of projects of different types."

To foster greater awareness of your situation, consider these practical tips:

1. Consult with a mentor or coach with experience and knowledge in a similar field or situation.

2. Network and connect with others in your industry or community.

3. Read relevant books, articles, and blogs to stay informed on the latest trends.

4. Invest in your personal and professional development through relevant classes or workshops.

5. Collaborate with others for different perspectives and innovative solutions.

6. Get feedback from friends, family, colleagues, or even customers.

7. Seek out diverse perspectives to encourage diversity of thought.

These steps will help you gain a wider range of insights that can better inform your decisions. The more you understand your situation from different angles, the better equipped you will be to move forward confidently.

"The term planning fallacy [describes] plans and forecasts that are unrealistically close to best-case scenarios."

-- DANIEL KAHNEMAN,
THINKING, FAST AND SLOW

Communicate Carefully and Make Amends

Effective communication forms the backbone of the Reputation Triage process. It plays a pivotal role in mending relationships, resolving conflicts, and reaching mutually beneficial agreements. Here are some suggestions to refine your communication skills:

- Practice active listening: Make a conscious effort to understand the perspectives and feelings of others. This builds trust.

- Prioritize understanding: Strive to understand others' perspectives and needs and find common ground.

- Reach agreements: Negotiate effectively and be willing to compromise to find solutions that meet everyone's needs.

- Use clear language: Avoid jargon to ensure your message is understood.

- Avoid blaming: Don't blame or shame others. Instead, focus on root cause solutions.

By adhering to these suggestions, you can restore trust in your leadership, enhance your relationships, and lead a more fulfilling life.

Do Not Lie, Blame, or Shame

Avoid lying, blaming, or shaming at all costs. These behaviors damage your reputation and leadership. Instead, accept responsibility, communicate effectively, and work towards solutions. The buck stops with you as a leader, and shaming others merely fosters fear and mistrust, crippling relationships and communication. Maintain your integrity and regain trust by focusing on solutions and effective communication.

Separate and Sort

Managing the Reputation Triage process requires careful organization and prioritization. A practical way to achieve this is by creating four lists: 'Now,' 'Next,' 'Later,' and 'Never.' Allocate tasks and conversations based on their urgency and importance, allowing you to manage your time effectively and address the most pressing issues first.

An Effective Method

To fully appreciate the efficacy of the Reputation Triage process, consider at the example of Johnson & Johnson during the Tylenol crisis in 1982. When seven people died after taking Tylenol capsules laced with cyanide, Johnson & Johnson admirably adhered to the principles of the Reputation Triage process.

Even though they didn't have to, Johnson & Johnson acted swiftly to remove 31 million bottles of Tylenol from the shelves, resulting in a loss of more than $100 million dollars.

They accepted full responsibility, conscientiously communicated with the public, did not lie, blame, or shame, and brought awareness to the situation. Even though their reputation was on the line, they prioritized consumer safety above all, demonstrating their integrity. They rebuilt their reputation, and today, Tylenol continues to be a trusted brand worldwide.

In summary, the Reputation Triage process is about assessing the severity of the situation, prioritizing recovery actions, leveraging outside perspectives, and most importantly, leading with integrity and responsibility.

As we face crises or challenges that impact our reputation, it is these principles that will guide us to resolution and recovery. Following the Reputation Triage process is an effective way station on your trek from setback to comeback.

The priority you place on any given element in this process will depend on your specific circumstances and values. Remember, however, that none of the elements in the process should be overlooked or disregarded in your efforts to restore a damaged reputation. Only when you restore your reputation will others have the confidence in your leadership required for you to effectively lead again.

KEY TAKEAWAYS

- Always assess the severity and potential impact of a situation before it escalates. Use a severity scale to determine the level of response required.
- Identify the immediate and necessary actions to be taken. This includes communication, operational adjustments, and other relevant changes.
- Seek advice from outside experts for new insights. This can provide objective insights and recommendations to navigate the situation more effectively.
- Lead with integrity and take responsibility, even if it means short-term loss. This is critical for long-term reputation recovery and building trust with stakeholders.
- Open, transparent, and regular communication with all stakeholders is crucial to manage and mitigate any damage to reputation.
- Every crisis is a learning opportunity. Identify key lessons and incorporate them into future crisis management plans.

ACTION ITEMS

- Develop a framework for assessing potential crises in terms of their severity and impact on reputation. This should be applied regularly and especially when potential issues arise.
- Create a crisis management team responsible for identifying and implementing recovery actions. Ensure that this team is well-equipped and trained.
- Build relationships with external advisors or consultants who can provide a fresh perspective during a crisis. Have them on standby and ready to assist when needed.
- Cultivate a corporate culture that prioritizes integrity and responsibility. Provide training to employees and leaders on ethical decision-making and accountability.
- Develop a communication strategy for crisis situations. This includes a plan for regular updates, and who should communicate on behalf of the company.
- After any crisis or potential reputation-damaging event, conduct a post-mortem analysis to extract key lessons. Update the crisis management plan accordingly.

CHAPTER 8

The Leader's Lens

Refocusing After Unforeseen Setbacks

Leadership can be a challenging journey, filled with unexpected turns. Sometimes, unexpected events blindside us. These are our "blind spots," unrecognized weaknesses or threats that can hinder our success.

Let me share a personal story that illustrates the concept of being blindsided and the process of bouncing back.

I was married for fifteen years, and despite the usual ups and downs, I believed our marriage was strong. Then, one day, I came home to find my wife had moved out and filed for divorce. I was completely blindsided. I knew we had been facing challenges, but I had no idea things had reached that point.

The shock was devastating. The love of my life had ripped out my heart, torn it to shreds in front of me, and set the pieces on fire. I was in a state of absolute shock, abject horror, and complete dismay, not just because it was happening to *me*, but because I viscerally felt the impact this event would have on *our son*, who was two-and-a-half-year-old when this happened.

When I say I was in a state of shock, I mean I went into actual, physical and psychological shock. I collapsed on my kitchen floor. I remember thinking, "This is how I die." It literally felt like my body was actually dying. My chest hurt, and I couldn't breathe normally. I've never felt anything like it.

The physical toll was immense, and immediately I found myself in a state of physiological shutdown. For two days, I was unable to eat, drink, or sleep. I had food-poisoning like symptoms. I wept almost constantly.

After around 44 hours of this, my condition had become life-threatening. I managed to get myself to a medical spa operated by a friend of mine, a registered nurse. She gave me two bags of I.V. fluids, with vitamins, electrolytes--the works. I remember her saying, "Noel, you need to go to the doctor. You're dangerously dehydrated. Another day or two of this, and you'll be dead."

Those words still echo in my ears. Her sobering warning underscored the severity of my condition. I took her advice, and got medical treatment for my symptoms. Even though I was never formally diagnosed with takotsubo cardiomyopathy, or "Broken Heart Syndrome," I had all the symptoms of the condition.

I was less than two days from death from grief. Over the next three weeks, I lost 20 lbs (9.07 kg). Physically recovering from this extreme trauma took several months. The emotional healing, by the grace of God, is ongoing, but I am far better, and following the lessons that have become parts of this book, along with the support of the people who I've recognized in this books Acknowledgements section, helped me recover far more quickly than I ever would've expected.

My wife's sudden betrayal hit me in a blind spot created by my love for her and my belief that the strength of our shared values was enough to sustain our marriage through any difficulty. I had to learn the hard way that nothing, not even a marriage to someone who says they share your faith and commitment to a shared vision for family is above ongoing rational scrutiny.

I want to add that, despite the horrific nature of this experience, the divorce was a catalyst for radical personal growth and healing. In the time that followed, I rebuilt myself, redoubled my efforts to promote healthy relationships in my life, and revitalized my professional life. I learned that even in the face of unspeakable personal loss and emotional devastation, it's possible to not only survive but to thrive.

Even in light of the profound upheaval and sorrow brought about by our separation, I still hold a deep and enduring love for my wife. This ordeal, though fraught with pain and turmoil for myself, our son, and our extended family, has not extinguished the flame of deep love that I bear for her. I acknowledge that our divorce, a path I cannot reconcile as necessary or fitting, nonetheless remains a part of our shared history. In this, I am steadfast in my pursuit of compassion and understanding towards her perspective. My commitment to forgiveness, healing, and the hopeful prospect of reconciliation remains unwavering. This chapter in our lives has imparted a crucial lesson: the realization that control over life's outcomes and circumstances is an illusion. It is in my response to these challenges where my true agency lies, guided by grace and a heart seeking peace.

Many of the lessons I've shared in this book are the result of this journey of recovery and growth. Much of the reason I have written this book, in fact, is because I believe many of the readers of this book have faced challenges as daunting as mine. I want you to know that, not only are you not alone, but there actually is a genuine reason to continue hoping for a brighter tomorrow.

If, like me, you've been blindsided, you need to get past the fear of that kind of trauma catching you unaware, again. Being blindsided can be a traumatic experience, leaving you feeling vulnerable and uncertain. The rest of this chapter is written to help you do just that.

Without further ado, let's dive into one of the first steps to overcome them: improving our self-awareness.

Better Understanding Blind Spots

Blind spots are facets of our personality, behavior, or thinking that remain unseen to us but are evident to others. These can be unrecognized weaknesses, biases, or misconceptions we hold about ourselves. For instance, we might believe we're excellent listeners, while others perceive us as dismissive. Alternatively, we might underestimate our abilities in certain areas due to past experiences, despite evidence to the contrary. These blind spots can limit our growth and effectiveness as leaders, making it crucial to seek and accept feedback from others to uncover and address them.

However, it is important to remember that these are a normal part of the leadership journey, and there are steps you can take to overcome them and emerge stronger as a leader.

Blind spots, often unnoticed until too late, can silently threaten a leader's success. Common causes of blind spots include overconfidence, being overly positive, and power-related false perceptions. To overcome these blind spots, leaders can take a more introspective approach and audit their past mistakes, view their leadership from all angles, and cultivate an open culture that values vulnerability and encourages learning from mistakes. To foster an open culture, leaders should reduce review cycles, grant autonomy during review periods, and prioritize learning and insights over the setback of mistakes.

In pursuit of such a future, here are some insights to help you eliminate as many blind spots as possible, thereby reducing the odds of nasty surprises. They'll also help build resilience and determination in the face of future challenges.

See The Unseen

In his book, *Thinking, Fast and Slow*, Daniel Kahneman explores the inner workings of the human mind and how they affects decision making. He observes that many of our thoughts, impressions, intuitions, and decisions happen unconsciously, often before we are even aware of them. This can lead to critical thinking mistakes, but Kahneman provides insights for avoiding them more often.

Kahneman's insights are particularly relevant to the topic of recovering from a leadership setback. As leaders, it's important to understand the role that unconscious biases and thought processes play in our decision making. By becoming more aware of these processes, we can make more deliberate, thoughtful decisions and avoid mistakes that might otherwise hinder our success. By recognizing and addressing our unconscious blind spots, we can regain control and navigate challenges with greater success.

The human brain is programmed with biases and mental shortcuts, much of which operates unconsciously and is influenced by our environment. In fact, each second, only around 0.0011% of the information processed by the brain relates to the working of the conscious mind.

"The human brain can process up to 11 million bits of information per second. This is the natural processing capacity of the brain, including the conscious, subconscious, and unconscious mind. However, the conscious mind has a very limited capacity and it can handle anything from 40 to 120 bits of information in a second."[8]

This leaves a vast amount of thinking to the unconscious, making it difficult to eliminate blind spots in our thinking. Building rapport between your conscious mind and your unconscious mind, however, will help you challenge automatic thinking, adopt intentional thought patterns and actions, and, ultimately, disrupt unhealthy or undesirable habits, heuristics, and cognitive biases.

> "[Each] second, only around 0.0011% of the infor-
> mation processed by the brain relates to the working
> of the conscious mind."

Here are seven ways to disrupt your brain's autopilot and be more intentional in your daily thoughts and actions.

Improve Self-Awareness

Self-awareness is a crucial trait for leaders, particularly those seeking to uncover their leadership blind spots. The two categories of self-awareness psychologists often discuss are public self-awareness and private self-awareness. Public self-awareness focuses on how one is perceived by others, while private self-awareness focuses on how one perceives oneself.

In leadership, discussions often center on improving public self-awareness. This makes sense, as leaders are often concerned with how they are perceived by followers or potential followers.

To reveal blind spots, it's essential to focus on improving private self-awareness. This means having a clear and accurate perception of yourself, including being aware and accepting of your limitations.

One powerful example of the importance of self-awareness in leadership comes from Reed Hastings, the co-founder of Netflix. In 2011, Hastings made the decision to split Netflix's DVD and streaming services into separate businesses, a move that resulted in a pricing model that was not well received by customers. There was massive customer outrage, leading to a significant loss in subscribers.

In hindsight, Hastings admitted that he had not adequately considered how customers would react, revealing a blind spot in his self-awareness.

The Netflix incident underscores the importance of private self-awareness and understanding how our decisions might impact others. Leaders who are in tune with their strengths, weaknesses, and the potential consequences of their decisions can make more effective choices and reduce the likelihood of overlooking crucial factors.

Meditation is one way to explore your limitations and increase your self-awareness. Getting an outside perspective through therapy or seeking constructive criticism from a friend or colleague is also helpful. Having a different or more accurate perspective is key to short-circuiting automatic thinking and being more intentional in your thoughts and actions.

Being self-aware, in essence, is about breaking out of your comfort zone, a concept that leads us to the next strategy: intentionally encountering the unfamiliar.

Intentionally Encounter the Unfamiliar

Most people prefer familiar situations and shy away from unfamiliar ones. However, stepping out of your comfort zone can offer opportunities to think in new ways and disrupt your automatic thinking. This is where the wisdom of Richard Branson, the founder of Virgin Group, comes into play. Known for his adventurous spirit and willingness to take risks, Branson has ventured into a vast array of industries — from music to airlines to space travel.

His reasoning? Branson often cites the need to break the status quo and challenge the norm. One of his famous quotes sums it up well: "If someone offers you an amazing opportunity and you're not sure you can do it, say yes – then learn how to do it later!" This kind of thinking, while not always successful, has led to many innovative solutions and has made Virgin a powerful brand known for disruption.

Branson's willingness to venture into unfamiliar territories serves as an example for leaders who wish to break free from their comfort zones. By intentionally trying new things or approaching familiar activities differently, you can stretch yourself and gain fresh perspectives.

Starting small and taking low-risk steps is a good way to get started. Embarking on an adventurous hike, for instance, could provide a new perspective or develop your problem-solving skills in unexpected ways. Trying a new hike in a nearby park, instead of jumping into a challenging trek like Machu Picchu, might be a more efficient, if not more effective, way to embrace unfamiliar experiences.

As we become comfortable with the unfamiliar, it broadens our perspective and prepares us to embrace thought diversity - a crucial element in overcoming leadership blind spots. This aspect is discussed further in the next section.

Embrace Thought Diversity

In today's Western culture, the strongest influencers tend to focus heavily on biological diversity while neglecting the importance of thought diversity. This situation is tragic because thought diversity is the most critical kind of diversity, and its significance will continue to grow.

Take, for example, the story of Apple Inc. The company is renowned for its innovative products, and this innovation stems from its commitment to thought diversity. Steve Jobs, the company's co-founder, assembled a diverse team of thinkers for the Macintosh project, which included artists, engineers, and even an historian. By ensuring a variety of perspectives, Jobs helped create a groundbreaking product that forever changed the computing industry.

The success of Apple Inc.'s Macintosh project showcases the power of diverse thinking within a team. This commitment to embracing different ways of thinking underscores the transformative potential of thought diversity.

Thought diversity is becoming increasingly vital as our world evolves. As technology advances, our critical and creative thinking skills are becoming more important to solve problems and create solutions. With globalization connecting us in interdependent ways, understanding and embracing different perspectives and ideas is crucial for success.

Our understanding of the world and its complexities is growing, and to effectively tackle these challenges, we need a diverse range of viewpoints and approaches. Thus, thought diversity will only become more important in the future as the world becomes more complex and interconnected, and as our reliance on technology and critical thinking skills increases.

Harnessing thought diversity is instrumental in making data-driven decisions, which will be explored in the next section.

Meticulously Collect Information and Make Data-Driven Decisions

When making intuitive or emotional decisions, we often rely on our subconscious mind to process large amounts of data that our conscious mind can't handle efficiently. While this trust has its benefits, decisions that we want to make in a conscious and deliberate way should be based on facts that we can process effectively with our conscious mind.

Consider Amazon's decision to venture into cloud computing with the introduction of AWS (Amazon Web Services) in 2006. Amazon wasn't simply acting on a hunch. They meticulously collected and analyzed data, identified a significant business opportunity, and made a calculated decision to launch AWS. Today, AWS is a major profit center for Amazon, demonstrating the power of data-driven decisions.

Our brains use heuristic processes that can cause logically fallacious and biased thinking, which can negatively impact the quality of decisions based on them. The best decisions are those that are logically defensible. Your instincts may guide you in the right direction, but you should ensure you can logically defend your conclusions rather than acting solely on intuition.

Taking the time to critically analyze your decision-making process can help you avoid making a mistake by catching biases or fallacies. Therefore, it's crucial for leaders to make data-driven decisions and not let emotions cloud their judgment.

Remember, the quality of our decisions directly impacts the quality of our leadership, and therefore understanding our conative process, as discussed in the next section, becomes crucial.

Learn Your Conative Process and Avoid Making Decisions on Low Mental Energy

When we're tired, we're prone to making bad decisions. Fatigue can cloud our judgment and cause us to overlook important details. But did you know that there are different types of mental energy and that it's a finite resource that can be replenished?

Kathy Kolbe and her team of psychologists specialize in understanding the conative mind and how it operates. They describe how people's instincts and innate attributes define their natural method of operation (MO) and how to use it for increased productivity, comfort, and success. The Kolbe A Index® report reveals your daily mental energy budget, which can help you avoid decision fatigue and ensure the quality of your decisions. Understanding your MO and mental energy budget is key to making the most of your time and abilities.

Consider the example of Ernest Hemingway, the acclaimed American author. Hemingway followed a rigorous writing routine, getting up early in the morning to write, believing that his mental energy was at its peak then. He would work until he felt his mental energy waning, at which point he would stop for the day. This practice allowed him to consistently produce high-quality work throughout his career.

Remember, being aware of your own energy levels and planning accordingly can help you maintain the quality of your decisions throughout the day. As we turn to our next section on using the right tools, remember that good tools can help you manage your mental energy effectively.

Use Better Tools

Great craftsmen invest in a few great tools. Most don't tend to consider having top-of-the-line tools to be essential to doing great work, although in some cases, that is absolutely true. Rather, simply having high-quality tools is sufficient.

Having the right tools can make a big difference in your productivity and the quality of your work. Good tools can help you to consistently create great work, meet deadlines, and avoid frustration. However, it's important to keep in mind that having the best tools doesn't guarantee great work. The focus should be on what is essential, and it's okay to ignore everything else.

To illustrate this point, let's look at Pixar Animation Studios. Their movie, 'Toy Story', released in 1995, was the first entirely computer-animated feature film. At that time, computer animation was a relatively new tool in the movie industry. Despite the technological challenges, Pixar focused on the essential elements - compelling storytelling, memorable characters, and emotional depth. They didn't let the technology overshadow the art of storytelling. This balance resulted in a groundbreaking film that was a critical and commercial success, and paved the way for many more computer-animated films.

A word of caution is in order, though. Don't obsess over your tools. This can be one way that procrastination or a lack of creativity manifests. Focus on what is essential and don't get bogged down in details that aren't important to your work. Having the right tools will give you the confidence and capability to create great work, but the real focus should be on your skills and creativity.

Remember, as we move on to our next section on improving critical thinking, that no tool is as powerful as a well-honed mind.

Make an Effort to Improve Critical Thinking

If you review the previous suggestions, you'll notice that many of them focus on avoiding biases and logical fallacies. Blind spots can be caused by mental laziness or prioritizing convenience over accuracy. Good leaders should be dedicated to self-awareness and continuously improving their critical thinking skills.

One of the most notable examples of exceptional critical thinking in leadership is Elon Musk's application of "first principles" thinking. This method, which involves breaking a problem down to its most fundamental truths and then reasoning from there, allowed him to challenge traditional thinking in the automotive and aerospace industries. Rather than accepting the high costs of batteries, Musk reasoned from the basic elements, finding a new solution that made large-scale production of electric vehicles feasible. His approach to critical thinking propelled Tesla and SpaceX to the forefront of their respective industries.

Musk's distinctive method of thinking enabled him to disrupt various industries and foster innovation.

This real-life example shows that eliminating blind spots can sometimes require more than getting an outside perspective or taking a break to broaden your thought process. It often demands a conscious effort to change your thinking and break bad habits. This requires self-education, which many people shy away from due to the immediate effort required and the long-term nature of the benefits.

However, the rewards, as seen in Musk's case, are well worth the effort. Investing in improved critical thinking helps reduce blind spots and leads to better decision-making. Every leader should prioritize this for success.

Having developed robust critical thinking skills, we are now better prepared to face leadership setbacks. This brings us to an essential part of leadership - the bounce-back.

The Bounce-Back

Encountering a blind spot as a leader can be a jarring experience, a stark reminder of our inherent fallibility. However, it's important to remember that these instances don't spell the end of your leadership journey, especially when it comes to self-leadership. Rather, they represent critical moments of learning and growth.

Blind spots in leadership can indeed lead to unexpected setbacks, but they also offer invaluable opportunities for introspection and evolution. Acknowledging past mistakes, fostering an environment that values vulnerability, and perpetually learning, are the foundational stones upon which we can construct strategies to overcome these blind spots.

Throughout this chapter, we have explored the importance of improving self-awareness, delving into unfamiliar territories, embracing thought diversity, making data-driven decisions, and understanding our conative processes to conserve mental energy. We have highlighted the significance of adopting better tools to manage and curate information, and the need to make a conscious effort to enhance our critical thinking skills. All these steps are critical to overcoming blind spots and emerging as stronger, more resilient leaders.

Remember, setbacks are an intrinsic part of the leadership journey. It's through these setbacks, these blind spots, that we learn to better understand ourselves and our teams. Equipped with the right tools, mindset, and a spirit of resilience, you have the capacity to navigate any challenges that come your way.

In the end, it's not just about bouncing back. It's about using that momentum to propel yourself forward, using lessons learned to become more adaptive, compassionate, and effective leaders. Your leadership journey, marked by setbacks and triumphs, is a testament to your resilience. Armed with this deeper understanding of how to reduce and respond to blind spots, you are better prepared for whatever comes next on your leadership path.

KEY TAKEAWAYS

- Unexpected setbacks can occur in leadership due to blind spots, but they can be overcome by introspection, learning from past mistakes, and fostering an open culture that values vulnerability and learning.
- Unconscious biases and thought processes significantly influence decision-making. By becoming more aware of these processes, leaders can make more deliberate and thoughtful decisions.
- Improving private self-awareness, embracing thought diversity, making data-driven decisions, understanding your conative process, and continuously improving critical thinking skills are crucial for effective leadership.
- Setbacks are a normal part of the leadership journey. With the right tools and mindset, leaders can navigate challenges with resilience and determination.

ACTION ITEMS

- Audit your past mistakes and identify any blind spots in your leadership.
- Improve your private self-awareness and embrace thought diversity.
- Make data-driven decisions and understand your conative process to avoid decision fatigue.
- Invest in high-quality tools and make a conscious effort to improve your critical thinking skills.

CHAPTER 9

Tending the Inner Garden

A Leader's Approach to Boundaries

Boundaries, invisible yet crucial, form the lines on the map of our emotional landscape. Boundaries are not walls, though. Maintaining resilience as a leader involves actively promoting healthy, well-adjusted emotional relations between those closest to you and yourself. There is a balance between isolating and containing, on one hand, and creating breathing room and space to focus, on the other.

Just as a well-tended garden is crucial for a thriving environment, clear and established boundaries play a crucial role in maintaining a healthy relationship with others and your own emotional well-being. While the boundaries necessary to have breathing room and space to focus are essential, nothing in this chapter should be used to rationalize the creation of walls between you and anyone else. Walls are unhealthy. Boundaries are healthy.

In this chapter, we will delve into how to establish, maintain, enforce, and communicate healthy emotional boundaries, drawing lessons from prominent figures in Christian history and literature, to help you lead with confidence and competence, even in the face of unexpected challenges and obstacles.

Since no one can read your mind, it falls to you to openly express your insecurities, triggers, and other personal factors. This clarity helps prevent others from unintentionally infringing on the areas of your heart and mind that you wish to keep secluded. By upholding these clear demarcations, you safeguard both yourself and others from potential harm.

Even those closest to you may struggle to stay within your established boundaries. This is not a reflection of a lack of respect, but rather a result of their deep love and trust in you. Like a child, they may see only the beauty of your garden and not the hazards it may contain. It is important to gently remind them of the boundaries you have set and why it is important for both of you to abide by them.

When those closest to you disregard your boundaries, handle the situation with patience and kindness, as you would with a child. Correct them lovingly and remind them that the established boundaries in your relationship allow for peace and safety for both of you.

Into the Garden

"I passed by the field of a sluggard, by the vineyard of a man without sense; and lo, it was all overgrown with thorns; the ground was covered with nettles, and its stone wall was broken down."[9]

To cultivate a healthy and harmonious inner life, consider modeling your inner life after a well-tended garden.

This means taking responsibility for making your heart and mind as safe as possible and communicating any hazards or limitations to others. If you seek deep and meaningful connections with others, being introspective, intentional, mindful, and conscientious is essential.

It is equally important to be curious, considerate, respectful, and compassionate when interacting with others' gardens. Demonstrating that you can be trusted to respect their boundaries helps foster strong and meaningful relationships. By tending to your own garden, you attract others who will love, respect, and protect it.

Tending a Garden and Establishing Boundaries

Just as a well-tended garden requires hard work and dedication, the same can be said for fostering a healthy emotional framework. The soil must be nourished, the weeds must be pulled, and the plants must be tended to regularly to ensure they flourish. Similarly, to maintain our emotional well-being, we must nourish our self-understanding, weed out harmful influences, and regularly tend to our needs and values.

To appreciate this analogy on a deeper level, let's consider a powerful example from Christian history: Saint Ignatius of Loyola. Saint Ignatius, the founder of the Society of Jesus (Jesuits), formulated a set of structured prayers, meditations, and contemplative practices known as the 'Spiritual Exercises.' Carried out over a period of 28 to 30 days, these exercises provided a roadmap for deep self-reflection and discernment of God's will.

Much like a gardener who sets boundaries for his plants to grow and thrive, Saint Ignatius set spiritual boundaries through his Spiritual Exercises. He understood that structure and discipline, when combined with deep contemplation and openness to divine guidance, could lead to profound personal transformation and a closer relationship with God.

In our own lives, we may not set boundaries as strict as the Spiritual Exercises. However, the principle remains the same: establishing boundaries - whether emotional or spiritual - requires dedication, effort, and a constant practice of self-care and understanding. Just as Saint Ignatius did with his Spiritual Exercises, we too must formulate our own exercises for setting and maintaining our emotional boundaries. This could be in the form of regular self-reflection, open conversations with loved ones, or even setting aside dedicated 'me-time' every day.

Identifying and Setting Boundaries

Introspection and self-reflection are key in helping leaders to define and uphold sound emotional perimeters.

As we work on regulating and maintaining healthy relationships with our emotions, and seek to understand and set boundaries, a helpful resource is reflection on C.S. Lewis's insightful essay, "Men Without Chests," which appears in his excellent book, *The Abolition of Man*. In this essay, Lewis warns of a society producing leaders with developed minds and bodies but no 'chest' – that moral and emotional center, which balances our intellect and desires. Much like the emotional boundaries we discuss in this chapter, Lewis's "chest" symbolizes the essential fusion of reason and emotion, a sturdy moral compass guiding us through life's complexities.

As we develop into stronger leaders, let us strive not to become "men without chests," but individuals who harmonize reason and emotion within firm ethical boundaries, inspiring others with our resilience and empathy. Employing this essential blend of reason and emotion is the healthiest and best way to identify which boundaries are needed to safeguard our inner lives.

Setting boundaries is like drawing a map of your emotional landscape. Just as a gardener decides where to place their flower beds and how far the vegetables should be from the garden path, we need to decide which parts of our inner lives we wish to share and which we want to keep private. Such decisions are best made when hearts and minds are in balance and in agreement one with the other.

Communication is key in this step. By defining our emotional boundaries, we let others know what we consider acceptable behavior and which areas are off-limits. Clear communication helps avoid misunderstandings and unintentional harm.

As we delve into the process of setting and maintaining boundaries, let's take a look at a visual aid that simplifies these steps. I call it the 'Boundary Blueprint: A Four-Step Guide'. This blueprint encapsulates the journey of boundary management, starting from introspection and progressing to communication, enforcement, and continual reassessment.

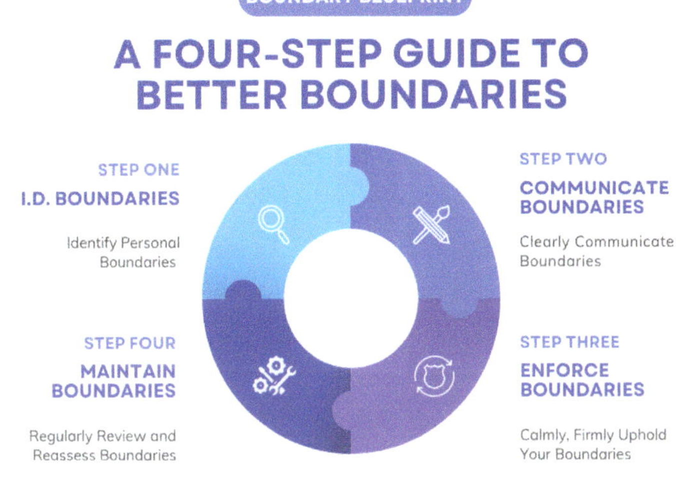

Enforcing Boundaries

Once we've set our boundaries, enforcing them becomes our next essential task. This process might mean reminding those closest to us about our boundaries, especially when they inadvertently wander across them, much like a child might wander into a garden without realizing the dangers it may contain.

In such instances, those close to us may not fully comprehend the emotional boundaries we have set. Therefore, it is important to gently guide them back to these boundaries.

We must remember that just as a gardener might erect a fence to protect their plants, we too must construct clear emotional barriers to safeguard our well-being. Also, like a gardener, we must ensure that our safeguards do not pose an unreasonable risk of harm to others.

Enforcing boundaries isn't about being punitive or simply pushing others away, but rather about nurturing mutual respect. Patience, understanding, compassion, and clear communication are key in this process, and they ensure that the importance of these boundaries is understood and respected by both parties.

Correcting with Love

A gardener not only nurtures and tends to their plants but also corrects their course when they stray.

A vine might need guidance with a trellis to grow in the desired direction, or a tree might need pruning to maintain its health. Likewise, setting emotional boundaries is not just about defining and protecting them; it's also about correcting course with love and compassion when those boundaries are crossed.

Saint Philip Neri offers a shining example of this approach. Known as the 'Apostle of Rome,' he was famous for his humor, humility, and knack for correcting others with kindness and love. He believed in gentle persuasion rather than harsh criticism, setting an example of how to enforce boundaries with grace and love.

In our own lives, it's important to remember that when someone crosses our emotional boundaries, it's often more productive to correct with love than to react harshly. Like Saint Philip Neri, we need to approach these situations with understanding, patience, and love.

Cultivating a Safe Environment

Maintaining a safe and conducive environment is an integral part of gardening. Gardeners provide their plants with appropriate amounts of water, ensure they get enough sunlight, and consistently monitor their growth.

Similarly, it's important for us to cultivate a safe emotional environment once we've set and protected our emotional boundaries.

Consider the example of Saint John Bosco, an Italian priest who dedicated his life to the betterment of disadvantaged youth during the 19th century. Bosco believed in providing a loving and supportive environment for his students, rather than relying on strict discipline or punishment. He created an emotionally safe space that fostered trust and respect, enabling the youth to grow and thrive.

In our lives, cultivating a safe emotional environment could involve surrounding ourselves with supportive relationships, engaging in activities we love, and allowing ourselves the time and space to reflect and heal. Like Saint John Bosco, we must foster a nurturing emotional environment where we can flourish.

Protecting the Garden

A gardener doesn't just tend to the growth of his garden; he also takes steps to protect it from harm, be it in the form of pests, severe weather, or intrusive animals. Similarly, in our emotional and spiritual lives, it's crucial to protect our boundaries and guard against external factors that could potentially harm our wellbeing.

To illustrate this point, consider the renowned Christian apologist and writer, C.S. Lewis. Despite the toll of losing his wife, Lewis didn't close himself off emotionally. Instead, he used his faith as a protective shield, allowing himself to grieve while not succumbing to despair. He was open about his pain and grief, thus protecting his emotional boundaries. He accepted his feelings, articulated them, and let them be a part of his life, demonstrating the importance of protecting our emotional boundaries even in the face of personal anguish.

In our own lives, protecting our emotional garden might involve creating a safe space for us to experience our feelings fully or seeking support during difficult times. Like Lewis, we must protect our emotional wellbeing, taking the necessary steps to ensure that our emotional boundaries remain intact.

By seeking refuge in daily prayer, participating in the Sacrament of Reconciliation, and receiving the Holy Eucharist, we can purify our hearts and receive the strong protection of God. By tending to our emotional garden, we attract others who will love, respect, and protect it just as we do.

"Our emotional boundaries are not cold, unyielding walls; they are the dappled, sunlit edges of our souls' gardens, delineating where we end and others begin."

Boundaries, Not Walls

In this discussion, we've mingled history mingles with legend and saintly whispers to unearth treasures both ancient and fresh. From vulnerability's humble strength to the reflecting pool's calming wisdom, we've gleaned truths that stretch far and wide like the roots of an ancient tree.

Let's pause for a moment and sit by that reflecting pool. Recall, if you will, the soft ripples of our discussion on how self-scrutiny can unveil the hidden chambers of our hearts. By understanding our shadows, we allow the light to touch them, and in so doing, we are able to speak our truths. A word shared in earnest can defuse a storm, can't it? It's a simple remedy, yet profound in preserving peace within and without.

Consider the saints and writers who have trod this path before us. Think of Saint Ignatius of Loyola's quest, Saint Philip Neri's joy, Saint John Bosco's love, and C.S. Lewis's imaginative faith. Our emotional boundaries are not cold, unyielding walls; they are the dappled, sunlit edges of our souls' gardens, delineating where we end and others begin. This isn't a mere philosophy; it's a living truth, isn't it?

Leadership, my friends, is no mere task or title. It's an art, a gentle tending to the gardens of our souls. By pruning here and planting there, we nurture resilience. Ah, resilience! It's like a fine wine, nourishing and invigorating, enabling us to dance through storms with a heart light and free.

As we look through the window of these luminous lives, what a view we behold! Emotional boundaries emerge not as grim barriers but as loving companions. They stand as robust trellises guiding our relationships, the fertile soil feeding our dreams, and the soothing shade under which we rest.

The path to resilient leadership? It's not hidden; it's illuminated in the gentle light of wisdom. It's carved with deep thought, lined with reflective beauty, and protected by those faithful boundaries. And as we walk, let's carry the lanterns of saints and authors. Let their words be our melody, singing us toward a leadership not only of success but of heart and soul. A leadership that echoes in the laughter of children, that warms the hand of a friend, and that kindles the fires of love and life itself. That's a leadership worth pursuing, don't you think?

KEY TAKEAWAYS

- Establishing and maintaining healthy emotional boundaries is crucial for resilience in leadership and personal well-being.
- Clear communication of personal boundaries is essential to prevent misunderstandings and potential harm.
- Emotional boundaries should be enforced with patience, kindness, and understanding, similar to how a gardener tends to their garden.
- Introspection and self-reflection are key in identifying and communicating personal boundaries, and they contribute to resilience in leadership.

ACTION ITEMS

- Reflect on your personal boundaries and identify any areas that need clearer communication or enforcement.
- Practice communicating your boundaries clearly and unambiguously to those around you.
- When boundaries are crossed, respond with patience and kindness, explaining the importance of the boundary for both parties.
- Regularly engage in introspection and self-reflection to maintain awareness of your emotional boundaries and to foster resilience in your leadership role.

CHAPTER 10

The Garden and the Fortress

Balancing Healthy Boundaries and Disarming Harmful Barriers

RETURNING TO THE WELL-TENDED GARDEN

In the last chapter, I used the metaphor of a well-tended garden to describe the process of establishing, communicating, enforcing, and maintaining the healthy boundaries necessary for a balanced and vibrant inner life. In this chapter, we will continue to employ this metaphor as we examine the potential dark side of boundaries.

Having balanced, clearly-communicated, compassionately enforced, and reasonably maintained boundaries can be a sign of self-respect. Such boundaries can ensure interactions are mutually respectful, caring, and appropriate. An often neglected topic in discussions of emotional boundaries, however, is the weaponization of boundaries, when ostensibly innocuous safeguards become danger-ous psychological weapons.

Rigidly enforced boundaries are only required when a person has not demonstrated their willingness and ability to safely accompany you as a trustworthy and careful co-custodian of your inner life.

When someone has demonstrated their commitment to making a decent effort to be a safe and respectful guardian, enforcing rigid boundaries towards them is a sign of paranoia. It is a loss of ability to differentiate between friends and foes, treating someone who is supportive as a threat. This behavior can result in pushing away those who care for us and causing further isolation, which can be emotionally harmful for both parties involved.

"Weaponizing boundaries," is not just a clinical term; it's a painful reality. Boundaries are weaponizing when limits, ostensibly meant to protect oneself, are turned against others, becoming in-struments of harm, rather than necessary safeguards.

Rather than serving as necessary protective measures to main-tain personal well-being and healthy relationships, these supposed "boundaries," which are not true boundaries at all but, rather, dangerous psychological traps, become tools to manipulate, control, and harm others. Metaphorically, speaking, this is like digging pitfall traps throughout your garden into which an unsuspecting person might fall and suffer injury. Weaponizing boundaries are distortions of what healthy boundaries are meant to be.

Self-awareness is your most important asset as you work to balance your efforts to maintain healthy boundaries without weaponizing them. As we further our examination into the nature of weaponized boundaries, let us explore the circumstances in which protective measures can become psychological weapons.

When Boundaries Become a Weapon

The garden metaphor takes a darker turn when we examine the scenario in which boundaries are not merely barriers but weapons. In our garden, this sinister transformation turns protective hedges into barriers of sharpened blades, a process that begins with a descent into paranoia and evolves into an even more harmful mindset characterized by defensive aggression.

Paranoia's rigid enforcement can lead to a disturbing alienation that harms not only the one harboring these fears but also those committed to being caretakers of their inner lives. This is where the garden's protective barriers become sharpened blades, cutting off connection and understanding.

Stonewalling, a toxic way of enforcing boundaries, emerges from this paranoia. Like its name suggests, stonewalling is akin to erecting a high wall of stone that blocks the light of love that otherwise might promote healthy growth in one's inner garden. Stonewalling blocks growth and withers connections. Notice, stonewalling represents an unhealthy retreat—a withdrawal into the garden's shadows, where emotions wither and communication breaks down. When someone stonewalls, they disengage, they avoid, they flee from connection. It's a mechanism that might temporarily shield from perceived threats but ultimately corrodes the soul of the relationship.

Defending this behavior as merely "maintaining boundaries" leads to self-deception or even passive-aggressive manipulation. It's a denial of the space emotions need to breathe, leading to a vicious cycle that festers and darkens the garden's vibrant hues.

> **"Stonewalling, a toxic way of enforcing boundaries, emerges from ... paranoia."**

Stonewalling is a painful coping mechanism, but sometimes it's a sign of something even more concerning. It can be an alarm, pointing to deep-seated issues that require attention and care. In extreme instances, stonewalling may be a sign of something deeper, something painful and complex, such as control issues or personality disorders like borderline, narcissistic, or anti-social personality disorder. These aren't just clinical terms; they're real struggles that need compassion and professional guidance.

Weaponizing boundaries through harmful behaviors, such as stonewalling, are manifestations of mistrust and fear which have metastasized into a deeper, even more concerning condition: paranoia. This isn't merely a garden's shadow, but a pestilence that affects the entire landscape of our emotional well-being.

Paranoia Is a Problem

Paranoia is not just a clinical term or a fleeting fear; it's a shadow in our garden, but a weed that, if left unattended, can choke the life out of our emotional landscape. A paranoid mind perceives a warped, distorted version of the world, making that which ought to appear innocuous feel threatening and harmful. It's a personal struggle that can feel overwhelming and isolating.

A gardener facing broken trust may feel the urge to barricade the garden, to fortify the walls to an extent where not even a gentle breeze can caress the blossoms within. But this affirmation of paranoid thoughts can yield destructive consequences for both the enforcer of these boundaries and those against whom they're unjustly wielded.

The answer is not to build higher walls but to cultivate a space where open and fair communication can flourish. Friends, family, and those we hold dear must become gardeners together, tending to the wounds, fostering growth, and perhaps seeking professional guidance if the garden becomes too overgrown with mistrust.

While paranoia can cast a shadow over our inner garden, there is a path through the fear and mistrust. There is a way to get back into the nurturing light of emotional intimacy. Walking together, hand-in-hand through the well-tended garden of our hearts is possible, and returning to that shared vision is the uplifting note on which we'll finish our discussion of boundaries.

Walking Together in the Well-Tended Garden: Navigating Emotional Intimacy

Emotional intimacy, like walking hand-in-hand through a well-tended garden, is a path paved with effort, affection, and mutual growth, where every step nurtures a shared commitment. It's an adventure into the vibrant landscape of the human soul, filled with complexities and rewards.

As we strive to heal and evolve from our setbacks, strong, profound relationships become the fertile soil from which we blossom. These connections demand our care, our empathy, and a willingness to face challenges together. The path may sometimes be strewn with thorns, but the destination is a shared sanctuary filled with love, respect, and trust.

Our world often conditions us to be guarded, watchful for threats that may lurk around every corner. But must we forever be gardeners in armor? Our emotional boundaries are not cold, unyielding walls; they are the dappled, sunlit edges of our souls' gardens, delineating where we end and others begin. To walk hand in hand with those we cherish, we must sometimes lower our shields, trusting in the goodness we see in one another.

Research points to a delicate balance in our interactions: for every storm that might assail our garden, several gentle rains of positivity are needed to restore equilibrium.[10] This balance emphasizes the need to nurture positive experiences in our relationships and to mend any breaks with care and urgency.

The intimate moments, the shared laughter, the unspoken understanding—all these are the treasures of our gardens. Cultivating resilient relationships that bring us joy and growth is not a mere task; it's an essential part of our journey towards recovery, fulfillment, and love.

KEY TAKEAWAYS

- Healthy boundaries are crucial for self-respect and mutual respect in relationships, but rigid enforcement can be a sign of paranoia.
- Stonewalling, or emotional withdrawal, is a harmful coping mechanism that disrupts effective communication and relationship building.
- Paranoia and stonewalling leads to isolation and emotional harm. When it these patterns of behavior are habitual, they are a form of psychological abuse, and should be addressed with open communication and professional help, if a person cannot or will not break the patterns on their own.
- Cultivating strong, meaningful relationships and promoting positive interactions are key to personal and professional recovery.

ACTION ITEMS

- Reflect on your own boundaries and consider whether they are being enforced in a healthy or paranoid manner.
- Identify any instances of stonewalling in your interactions and consider healthier ways to cope with negative emotions.
- If paranoia or stonewalling is causing harm in your relationships, seek professional help, and engage in open communication to address the issue.
- Make an effort to cultivate strong relationships and promote positive interactions as part of your recovery journey.

CHAPTER 11

Reinvention Is the Intention

It's Time for You X.0

Reinvention is a journey that we all undertake multiple times throughout our lives. It can be triggered by a major life change, such as starting school, getting a job, getting married, or moving to a new place. As you read this book, you may be in the midst of reinventing yourself after a personal or professional setback.

Regardless of the reason, reinventing yourself requires effort, care, and a commitment to growth. Rather than merely trying to leave the past behind and defining yourself exclusively by your response to a milestone in your life, an endeavor as foolhardy to attempt as it is impossible to accomplish, reinvention is a continuous process of upgrading your understanding of yourself.

This is not an overnight transformation, and the process of re-invention will require a great deal of effort and patience before you start to really recognize the new version of yourself as having largely replaced the old version.

If you're familiar with the Ship of Theseus, a thought experiment first posed by the ancient Greek philosopher Plutarch, you'll have a sense of what the process looks like. In the thought experiment, the famous ship sailed by the hero Theseus is preserved by gradually replacing each damaged plank as it begins to rot, until no original plank remains. This raises the question - is it still the same Ship of Theseus if all its parts have been replaced?

In the same way, by continuously working to upgrade your mindset, values, beliefs, habits, and skills through the reinvention process, you are replacing the 'planks' that comprise who you are. At the end of this journey, the new 'planks' may add up to a very different version of yourself. But like the ship, you are still you even if the parts have changed. There won't be two versions of you, except in your memory and the memories of those who knew you before.

The process of reinvention involves two phases: the mindset phase and the operative phase. In each phase, there are six steps that will help you on your journey. Here's a breakdown of the reinvention process:

Mindset Phase

1. Know Thyself
2. Surface Core Values
3. Free Up Resources
4. Check In and Record Reflections
5. With a Trusted Advisor, Evaluate Strengths & Weaknesses
6. Experiment

Operative Phase

1. Visualize Your Aspirations
2. Establish a Reliable Support Network
3. Engage in Lifelong Learning
4. Experiment Bigger
5. Employ a Process of Reflection, Self-Assessment, and Responsive Action
6. Celebrate Little (and Big) Wins

In this chapter, I'll take you through each step of the process and show you how to build the habit of reinvention. This chapter is a bit longer than others in this book, because, like you, I recognize that the process of reinvention is as essential as it is difficult.

As you engage with this work, the most important thing to remember is that every directionally correct step you take is a win, regardless of your degree of perceived success immediately following your attempt. Often, results take time. So, let's get started on your journey of self-reinvention, starting with the Mindset Phase of the process.

MINDSET PHASE

Know Thyself

The first step is introspection - taking time to deeply understand your values, passions, strengths and weaknesses. In 2005, I studied abroad in Greece with Professor of Classics, Dr. Timothy Winters, who took us to the Temple of Apollo at Delphi, at the entrance of which is inscribed the ancient Greek aphorism: "KNOW THY-SELF." This ancient wisdom has guided and challenged me since I first encountered it, inspiring me to pursue self-awareness not as an egotistical exercise but in order to better understand myself as a person passionate about connection with others.

Introspection is difficult, as we are always changing and never fully know ourselves or others. But acknowledging our limited beliefs and knowledge is the beginning of wisdom and self-awareness. Owning our limitations, across physical, cognitive, emotional and spiritual dimensions, is also key.

Empathy and compassion provide insight into how others see us, highlighting our blind spots. Approach self-discovery with radical honesty - letting go of who you *want to be* and accepting *who you are,* right now. For example, after a painful breakup, I took time to reflect and more deeply appreciate how and why my faith, close family, and friends were the most important parts of my experience of life. Reinventing myself involved prioritizing these relationships, not just in terms of how I felt, inside, but in terms of how I showed up in others' lives.

Without self-awareness, intentional reinvention will be challenging, if not impossible. Useful introspective exercises include journaling, meditation, and candid discussions with trusted advisors. Mitchell S. Green, a prominent modern philosopher and Professor of Philosophy at the University of Connecticut, known for his insights into the nature of expression, self-knowledge, and the philosophy of language, once said, "It seems to me the beginning of wisdom of any kind, including knowledge of ourselves, is acknowledgment of the infirmity of our beliefs and the paucity of our knowledge."

His words provide a profound foundation for understanding the complexities of self-awareness and growth.

By blending introspective practices with radical honesty, you can uncover your authentic self - a crucial foundation for reinvention. Remember, this first step on the journey requires acknowledging your imperfect self-knowledge. With an open and curious mindset, you're ready to start understanding your multidimensional self on a deeper level. This begins with a close examination of your core values and most enduring desires.

Surface Core Values

Discovering your core values is a crucial step in reinventing yourself, as they give you purpose and direction. However, this can be challenging, especially after a setback has shaken your sense of self.

Useful introspective exercises include reflecting on times when you felt most authentic, actions taken out of strong conviction, and who you admire and why. For example, as I reflected on my relationships with those who have had the most profound impact on me throughout my life, I realized generosity, growth, and creativity were core values based on my attraction to role models who embodied these qualities.

Assessments can help reveal your values. However, I recommend collaborating with a coach or mentor for the most insightful discoveries. Their outside perspective can challenge assumptions we hold about ourselves. Don't take shortcuts here! This work lays the foundation for your reinvention journey.

To guide your reflection, consider:

- When have you felt compelled to speak or act? What tends to motivate such a response, and, in those moments, what have you been willing to sacrifice?
- Who do you admire and why? How do you aspire to match or exceed their qualities?
- Recall moments of authenticity, success and confidence. What actions did you take? Who supported you? What results did you hope to achieve?

After reflecting, identify your top values and record them. Let these values direct you as you reinvent yourself. Remember, bringing your authentic core values to the surface is well worth the effort and self-examination. With clarity on your purpose and direction, you can build the life you want on a solid foundation.

The key to all this is asking insightful questions to reveal values hidden beneath the surface. When you can do that, you'll have more confidence that you're on the right path. I can't stress enough how important it is to be radically honest with yourself during this reflective process. A mentor can provoke deeper self-discovery by challenging your assumptions. With core values as your compass, you can navigate change and growth with confidence.

Free Up Resources

To reinvent yourself, you will likely need to intentionally create space. Declutter your schedule, environment and mind to uncover the new you waiting to emerge.

For example, I have adjusted my use of social media and have been highly selective about making new commitments, avoiding burn-out. Greg McKeown's book *Essentialism* provides useful strategies for identifying non-essential distractions and obligations.

Understanding your mental energy budget using tools like the Kolbe A™ Index is also enlightening. This reveals when you have the most motivation and stamina for focused work. McKeown's book *Effortless* further explores accessing your innate abilities for reinvention.

Clearing clutter enables you to rearrange the pieces of your life into the new picture you desire. Who do you want to become? Re-invention requires editing and refining until your life reflects your aspirational identity.

Practice mindfulness to quiet your mind. Streamline your schedule to create time for what matters. Remove physical clutter hindering clear thought.

By freeing up mental, emotional and physical space, you allow your authentic self to unfold. Don't forget to be present with intention, and take the opportunity, when it presents itself, to relish the lightness and freedom of simplified space. With a decluttered landscape (internal and external), your reinvention journey can truly begin.

With a Trusted Advisor, Evaluate Strengths & *Weaknesses*

Assessing your strengths and weaknesses is invaluable for re-invention, but can be challenging alone. Personality and strengths assessments like the Kolbe A™ Index or DISC provide useful snapshots, but avoid over-reliance on any self-evaluation. No single test defines your identity or abilities with certainty.

The most insightful discoveries come from collaborating with a trusted advisor, coach or mentor. Their outside perspective challenges assumptions we hold about ourselves. Feedback from my mentor helped me recognize strengths I had overlooked, like connecting with others on a human level.

With support, objectively evaluate your skills, knowledge, behaviors and attitudes. Be aware of tendencies towards extreme self-perceptions — positive or negative. The goal is balanced self-understanding, not justification of judgments and opinions of yourself.

Remember, the reinvention process is a journey, not a final verdict on your potential. Regular reassessment allows growth in self-knowledge as you change over time. Areas needing development today may become strengths tomorrow.

No test or advisor can provide the complete picture - only pieces to the puzzle. Synthesize insights from assessments and your support team to see yourself clearly. With awareness of your capabilities and limitations, you can craft an authentic vision for reinvention.

Leaning into your strengths while improving weaknesses, with the guidance of others, empowers meaningful transformation. Evaluating yourself through an objective lens is challenging but necessary work on the path of reinvention.

Experiment

Imagine you're Thomas, a corporate executive who's always felt drawn to the world of art. Your job pays well but doesn't ignite your passion. You've often found yourself pondering what life would be like if you pursued a career in painting.

Experimentation is the bridge from daydreaming to reality. For Thomas, the journey may begin with a low-risk experiment: signing up for an art class on weekends. Soon, his brush strokes may begin to reveal not just talent, but a profound connection to a world he'd never fully embraced.

This small step may illuminate a path. Thomas may start collaborating with local artists, immersing himself in a creative community, and testing out part-time roles in galleries. Each experiment is like a puzzle piece, fitting into a new identity that resonates with his true self.

Through this illustration, we can see that reinvention isn't just a sudden leap but a series of courageous steps outside the comfort zone. You, too, can start small. If you've crafted a hypothesis like "By living more authentically, I'll inspire others to work together to accomplish goals we share," then test it!

Try new activities that align with your interests. Volunteer in fields that intrigue you. Engage your family in new shared adventures. Each experiment is a chance to learn, to grow, and to inch closer to the 'you' you want to become.

Not every step will be a home run, and that's okay. Each Thomas will have his share of false starts and disappointments, but an open and curious mindset will turn every stumble into a learning opportunity.

Keep exploring and follow what energizes you. Embrace surprises and remember, the path to reinvention is a thrilling journey filled with insights, alignment, and self-discovery. Your future awaits, and it starts with the courage to experiment.

"Know Thyself"
-- ANCIENT GREEK PROVERB

Check In and Record Reflections

As you reinvent yourself, regularly record reflective journal entries to cement insights and track your evolution. Personally, I have shared much of my process publicly, intentionally offering others evidence that healing is possible. In 2021 and 2022, as I was rebuilding myself in the wake of profound personal tragedies, I even did this by posting about what I was going through on social media.

Sometimes we heal in public so the ones doing it in private can keep going. This level of vulnerability and openness is not for everyone, though.

Choose whatever style works for you - private journaling is just as valid. Be honest yet gentle in your reflections. Note feelings that come up, how behaviors align with values, when old patterns persist or new habits emerge. Share what you are comfortable with. There is vulnerability in transparency, but also power in the radical accountability that comes along with such openness.

Resist harsh self-criticism, instead focusing on constructive lessons and positive changes underway. As your reinvention unfolds, self-reflection builds self-awareness and accelerates growth.

For instance, carefully reflecting on my lifelong efforts to pursue connections with others and proactively repair ruptures whenever they happen revealed that, while I have made mistakes, I am not ultimately responsible for the state of relationships that have taken a dark turn in my life. I have had to accept that two people are required to make or break a relationship, and I cannot make things better, alone. I've blamed myself whenever others have been unwilling or unable to match my desire and effort to grow together or to reconcile after damage has been done to the relationship. Reflective writing provided me with clarity not only on what drives my authentic self by the limits of what is possible and what I should expect from my efforts.

Such realizations frequently happen when you take time to revisit your entries, checking on your progress over time. These notes chart your odyssey of self-discovery, reminding you how far you've come. Noticing incremental changes builds motivation to continue reinventing yourself.

Whatever form feels right, make reflection a touchpoint throughout your process of change. Self-examination is the compass guiding your reinvention journey. Record, review and integrate insights to manifest your highest potential. Within you, is greater wisdom than you may realize.

OPERATIVE PHASE

Visualize Your Aspirations

The operative phase starts by visualizing your aspirations for reinvention in concrete detail, which makes them seem more achievable. Consider what your mornings, workdays, evenings, weekends, and vacations will look like after your reinvention efforts have started yielding more predictable outcomes than learning opportunities. Envision specific routines, activities, projects and quality time.

In addition to visualizing the future, make a list of specific goals across health, career, relationships and other areas, keeping it essential. Focus on what you truly need to gain unshakable confidence in your reinvented self. How long your list is depends on your specific situation and objectives.

Then, make an essentialized list of S.M.A.R.T. goals - Specific, Measurable, Achievable, Relevant and Time-Bound - across the key areas of your life.[11]

To make aspirations tangible, define and track quantitative metrics like energy, productivity, relationship satisfaction and progress on passion projects.

Bring your ambitions to life visually by creating vision boards or journals with inspiring images, affirmations and items symbolizing goals. Let these serve as daily motivation for incremental progress.

The more precisely you define and visualize your future self, the clearer the path to realization becomes. Combined with S.M.A.R.T. goal setting and measurement, you create a foundation for an attainable reinvented life.

Establish a Reliable Support Network

A reliable support network is invaluable for reinvention. Surround yourself with people who believe in your journey - mentors, coaches, friends and family. Throughout my own journey of rebuilding and reinventing, I have been blessed to have the guidance and support of a therapist, two trauma coaches, a clinical psychologist, a priest, several close friends, and my parents. Their unwavering encouragement and support has been instrumental in helping me overcome obstacles and become the thriving person I am today.

It's important to have people in your life who believe in you and your journey, so make sure to build and nurture a supportive network. Intentionally build your network by identifying two or three mentors who have successfully reinvented themselves. Their lived experience will provide invaluable guidance for your journey.

It's hard to overstate the value of collaboration. One unique voice that's echoed this wisdom is that of Helen Keller, an American author, political activist, and lecturer who was both blind and deaf. She is considered a pioneer in the education of persons with disabilities and is best known for her autobiography, *The Story of My Life*.

Keller was one of the first deaf-blind individuals to earn a bachelor of arts degree and is remembered for her inspiring speeches and activism on behalf of people with disabilities.

Keller famously said, "Alone, we can do so little; together, we can do so much." In life, especially as a leader, if you want to go far, you must learn to accept support.

Choose supporters who will challenge you with honesty, not just agreeability. Feedback from my wisest mentors pushed me to go further. Seek diverse perspectives to illuminate blind spots. Stay humble and open to counsel, even when difficult to hear. With guidance from your "reinvention board of directors," you can achieve far more.

In addition to mentors, consider establishing accountability partnerships with one or two trusted peers. Avoid surrounding yourself with people who will agree with everything you do. Instead, seek out constructive criticism from people who will firmly, fairly, and lovingly hold you to high standards. These can be some of the most beneficial kinds of support you receive from others.

Again, avoid echo chambers! Instead, aim to surround yourself with people who will challenge and support you. This is powerful, ancient wisdom. As we read in the book of Proverbs:

"Do not reprove a scoffer, or he will hate you; **reprove a wise man, and he will love you.**"[12]

"The way of the fool is right in his own eyes, but **a wise man listens to advice.**"[13]

To succeed in life, cultivate humility and acknowledge that you are not perfect, but that does not make you unworthy of love and acceptance. Instead, strive to get closer to perfection every day.

As Bruce Lee once said, "A goal is not always meant to be reached; it often serves simply as something to aim at."

In a support team member, what you want is someone who loves you, in the sense that they sincerely, altruistically desire what's best for you. "To love," after all, "is to will the good of the other."[14] Compassionately and clearly telling the truth is always a loving act, and refraining from doing so is always an unloving act.

Your support network should include people who will tell you things you may not want to hear and who you are willing to listen to. This may include mentors, coaches, therapists, mental health professionals, clergy, and wise family members.

Make sure the person giving you advice is loving, intelligent, and the right fit for the advice you're seeking. To this end, the Old Testament book of Sirach offers this insight:

"Do not consult with a woman about her rival or with a coward about war, with a merchant about barter or with a buyer about selling, with a grudging man about gratitude or with a merciless man about kindness, with an idler about any work or with a man hired for a year about completing his work, with a lazy servant about a big task—pay no attention to these in any matter of counsel."[15]

Focus on getting input from people who are subject matter experts! Find people who will encourage the new you and hold you accountable like mentors, coaches, supportive friends and family. My reinvention was aided tremendously by a priest friend and also by a mentor who has advised and motivated me.

Finally, consider joining (or starting) online or local reinvention-focused groups to connect with like-minded individuals. Doing so can generate both community and momentum. In these groups, as in your accountability partnerships, it's important to surround yourself with people who will be honest with you and tell you what you need to hear, not just what you want to hear.

Not all opinions are equally valid or useful, so it's important to seek out people who will challenge you and provide valuable insights. This will help you make the most of your conversations and support network.

Engage in Lifelong Learning

Continuous learning is integral to reinvention. Consider classes, workshops, events and books on personal growth. Leaders are readers and it's important to learn as much as you can about your strengths.

"The future belongs to the learners, not the knowers."
-- ERIC HOFFER

As philosopher Eric Hoffer identified, cultivating a beginner's mindset is key, recognizing there is always more to learn. Stay curious. Great leaders are devoted learners.

For example, lifelong learning completely transformed Ken Jeong's career trajectory. Already a practicing doctor, Jeong began taking improv and comedy classes out of curiosity. This led to performing stand-up, then acting roles, and ultimately his star turn in the "The Hangover" franchise.

Expanding your knowledge enables continuous renewal and evolution. Learning together with your support network also creates shared growth and momentum. So identify 2-3 books specifically focused on reinvention, leadership and goal achievement for you and your mentors to read and discuss.

Also engage in active learning by signing up for a course, such as a community class, a skill certification bootcamp or online learning. Look specifically for opportunities related to reinvention. Block out 15-30 minutes daily to devote to this structured learning. Consistency is key.

Experiment (Bigger)

In this stage, make a bold move that challenges you. Expand on the experiments you've been conducting during the Mindset Phase and aim for bigger goals aligned with your core values.

For example, address persistent personal issues holding you back or start a passion project on the side while maintaining your current work. Schedule specific hours for this that honor your mental energy budget.

In your career, explore stretch roles at work or leadership positions in volunteer organizations. Look for appropriate opportunities to apply for.

Take tangible steps to launch a small side business aligned with your interests and skills by developing a business plan. Enlist your accountability partner or online community to refine your ideas.

Committing to regular experimentation is invaluable, so keep piloting ideas before fully diving in. Embrace productive failure as a learning opportunity when experiments fizzle. Reflect on insights gained about your interests, skills and needs. Then refine your approach and continue iterating.

With an open and curious mindset, you will gain clarity on the path of reinvention. Keep exploring what energizes you until your experiments begin to reveal the authentic you waiting to fully emerge. The process of self-discovery is thrilling when approached as a journey, not a final verdict. Your future awaits; so, start experimenting (bigger), now!

Reflect, Assess, and Respond

Making time for consistent reflection and responsive action is key for reinvention. Set aside time each week to review your journal, check important metrics, and notice any stuck mindsets.

Pick some measurable goals around health, relationships, work, and personal growth. Then track data related to them like energy levels, productivity, new skills gained, and relationship satisfaction. Apps can automate the more tedious-seeming parts of this process. Review the metrics and make changes.

For example, rate your energy daily on a 1-10 scale. Use an app to track time spent in deep work. If productivity is lagging, try a new routine. Assess often and adapt.

Along with tracking habits, be vigilant to guard against limiting beliefs, such as perfectionism or imposter syndrome; these can sabotage your efforts. When they arise, intentionally adjust your self-talk with empowering affirmations.

Share lessons learned regularly with your accountability buddies and mentors. Ask for their feedback. Reinvention is about progress through continual small improvements, not instant perfection. Keep reflecting, assessing, and taking action to become your best self.

Throughout this part of the process, stay responsive. Use what you learn to iterate your approach. *Reinvention is not static, but an upward spiral of continuous improvement, reflection and action.* With each turn of the spiral, you integrate more of your authentic self.

Celebrate Little (and Big) Wins

When reinventing yourself, celebrate every small win. Mark milestones through meaningful activities that energize you. Keep celebrations proportional to the size and impact of the achievement.

Schedule regular victory celebrations into your calendar, such as a special meal out or tickets to an event you'll enjoy. Attach celebrations to specific goal progress markers.

Share wins with your support network. Let them know you appreciate their role in your journey. Celebrating together strengthens motivation and relationships.

Vocalize your progress and achievements by sharing on social media or community groups. This builds accountability and inspires others.

Keep a visualization journal with your goals and track wins as you make progress over time. Seeing your advancement motivates further improvement.

Celebrating small steps sustains the motivation needed for long-term reinvention. So commemorate every goal achieved, knowledge gained, and lesson learned. Stay encouraged remembering how far you've come.

UPGRADING TO YOU, VERSION X.0

The reinvention process begins by looking inward to assess your values, strengths, and aspirations. This self-awareness allows you to intentionally craft your ideal self.

Next, expand your comfort zone through continuous experimentation. Reflect on insights gained and refine your approach, supported by your trusted community.

Reinvention isn't instant perfection, but gradual betterment through ongoing small improvements. Adjust course frequently, integrate feedback, and celebrate every milestone.

You are continuously upgrading, becoming a better version of yourself with each iteration. There is no final verdict, only the endless opportunity for growth into your highest potential.

You now have the blueprint for reinvention and everything needed to manifest your goals. With an open mindset, your possibilities are infinite.

It won't always be easy, but challenges make the upgrades worthwhile. Have courage, stay curious, and don't stop striving. The summit is ahead and your legacy awaits.

You are ready to install V.X.0 - the next level of your best self. It's time for an upgrade!

KEY TAKEAWAYS

- Reinvention is a journey that requires effort, care, and commitment to growth. It involves two phases: the mindset phase and the operative phase, each with six steps.

- **The mindset phase includes the following steps:**

  - "Know Thyself": Acknowledge your limitations and understand yourself better through introspection.
  - "Surface Core Values": Identify your core values that give you a sense of purpose and direction.
  - "Free Up Resources": Create mental and emotional space for reinvention.
  - "Evaluate Strengths & Weaknesses": Understand your personal strengths and weaknesses, ideally with the help of a trusted advisor.
  - "Experiment": Test your hypothesis about who you want to become by trying out new activities or approaches.
  - "Check In and Record Reflections": Regularly record your reflections about your growth in a journal or diary.

- **The operative phase includes the following steps:**

  - "Visualize Your Aspirations": Create a list of your aspirations and make them as specific, measurable, achievable, relevant, and time-bound as possible.
  - "Establish a Reliable Support Network": Build and nurture a network of people who believe in you and your journey.
  - "Engage in Lifelong Learning": Cultivate a passion for learning and growing.

- "Experiment Bigger": Make a bold move that challenges you and aligns with your core values.
- "Employ a Process of Reflection, Self-Assessment, and Responsive Action": Track Key Performance Indicators (KPIs) that indicate your progress towards your goals and regularly check in with your support network.
- "Celebrate Little (and Big) Wins": Make time to celebrate your victories to stay motivated and move forward.

- Reinvention is about becoming the person you want to be, supported by a reliable network and a commitment to life-long learning.

ACTION ITEMS

- Spend some time in introspection to better understand yourself, your strengths, weaknesses, and core values. This could involve journaling, meditation, or even seeking feedback from those who know you well. Consider using tools like the Kolbe A™ Index or DISC assessment for a more structured approach.

- Write down a list of your aspirations, making them as specific, measurable, achievable, relevant, and time-bound as possible. This will help you visualize your goals and track your progress towards them.

- Identify individuals who can provide support, guidance, and constructive criticism on your journey of reinvention. This could include mentors, coaches, therapists, or trusted friends and family. Regularly check in with them for accountability and advice.

- Engage in activities that promote learning and growth. This could be reading books, attending seminars, or taking online courses. Additionally, take steps to experiment with new activities or approaches that align with your core values and aspirations. Remember to celebrate your wins, no matter how small they may seem, to keep yourself motivated and positive.

CHAPTER 12

Virtue in Leadership

The Path to Restoring Trust

In the United States and around the world, trust in public institutions is lower than it has been at any time since reliable records have been kept about the subject. The reason for this, I believe, is not because we have lost faith in ourselves or our fellow man, but because we have lost faith in our leaders. The lust for power exhibited by our leaders appears to outstrip, by a large margin, any desire they may have to do the right thing (assuming, of course, they would be able to identify *the right thing* if it sat on their faces).

One example of the disconnect between the expectations of leadership and the reality of it can be seen in the controversy surrounding the awarding of the Nobel Peace Prize to President Barack Obama in 2009. The Nobel Committee had hoped that the award would strengthen Obama's commitment to pursuing nuclear disarmament, but instead it was met with criticism from both supporters and critics alike. The former director of the Nobel Institute, Geir Lundestad, has since expressed regret and acknowledged that the committee didn't achieve what it had hoped for with the award.

This serves as a reminder of the importance of virtuous leadership and the need for leaders who not only make promises but also follow through on them with actions that align with their words.

Allow me to lighten the mood a little by sharing one of my all-time favorite quotes about government and leadership. It comes from *The Restaurant at the End of the Universe* by British humorist Douglas Adams, who also wrote the best-selling novel *The Hitchhiker's Guide to the Galaxy*. Adams wrote:

"The major problem—one of the major problems, for there are several —one of the many major problems with governing people is that of whom you get to do it; or rather of who manages to get people to let them do it to them.

To summarize: it is a well-known fact that those people who must want to rule people are, *ipso facto*, those least suited to do it. To summarize the summary: anyone who is capable of getting themselves made President should on no account be allowed to do the job. To summarize the summary of the summary: people are a problem."

Indeed, finding people who are both capable of leading and re-luctant-but-willing to lead has proven monstrously difficult. In the absence of such leaders, unpleasantly, we find ourselves faced with a rapid decline in trust in government.

"Pew Research Center has data on the amount of trust Americans have in their government to do what is right 'about always' or 'most of the time,' going back seventy years. In the 1950s, trust in government was high, at 73%. By the time Americans went to the polls to vote for Nixon, trust was down 11 points to 62% – due in large part to the conflict in Vietnam, showing what a large but policy-driven dip in trust can look like. By August of 1974 when Nixon resigned, just 36% of Americans had a high level of trust in the government.

Faith in our government to do the right thing never recovered. Trust eroded even further during the second half of the 1970s. For all of Reagan's optimism and 'reforming government' mantra, under his leadership trust in government never cracked 50%. In fact, it would reach levels on par with the 1950s and 1960s for only a brief moment – immediately after 9/11. Even that spike was short-lived, followed by a steady decline to 20% today."[16]

Our trust in government, now, is, in fact, lower than it was immediately after Watergate. The questions of why this is so and what, if anything, anyone can do about it are difficult to even ask, much less answer, in a meaningful way.

"[Our] declining trust in leaders and institutions right now is far more complex than simply feeling like you're not getting the whole story or the latest guidelines seem inconsistent with what you were told previously. It's really a matter of the psychological effects that compounded uncertainty has on our emotions. Our lack of trust stems from feeling vulnerable. And unfortunately, many Americans are feeling very vulnerable right now. So they look to their local chat groups instead of the WHO or life-long acquaintances instead of national scientific communities. They seek out similar-minded people on the internet and bond over their distrust and disdain for the leaders they don't know trying to tell them what to do."[17]

To improve leadership, we must reject moral relativism and embrace virtue. It's not enough for leaders to simply communicate effectively, be consistent, and refrain from rash decisions. We need leaders who set examples of how to be better. Virtuous leaders who display humility, charity, and self-sacrifice for the greater good build trust by demonstrating their reliable moral character through action.

Humility: The Chief Virtue of Leadership

People simply will not trust leaders whose morality is flexible or whose virtues seem to shift with the changing winds of public opinion. Therefore, humans need a settled, authoritative standard of moral and ethical behavior against which to judge individual leaders. It is in the consistent demonstration of humility, charity, and self-sacrifice that leaders prove they adhere to such a standard, thereby earning the trust and respect of those they lead. These virtues are not mere adornments but the very essence of virtuous leadership, with humility standing as the chief virtue guiding and informing all others.

> **"Happiness and moral duty are inseparably connected."**
>
> -- PRESIDENT GEORGE WASHINGTON

Never before has there been so much at stake. Never before have we had so little virtue, or needed it more, in our society. And the first virtue to which we should return is the one of which we find the least in modern culture: humility.

There is not a single uncharitable, unkind thing one person does to another person that isn't rooted in pride. "Haughty eyes and a proud heart, the lamp of the wicked, are sin." (Proverbs 21:4) Humility is the antidote to the toxicity of arrogance and entitlement that drives so much selfish, unkind behavior.

To improve leadership quality, society must reject moral relativism and embrace virtue. Living a virtuous life requires selflessness, humility, and patience. These traits can be cultivated over time by refocusing our instincts on social and transcendental goods.

George Washington gave us a great example of putting humility and self-sacrifice into action, as a leader. He famously said, "Happiness and moral duty are inseparably connected." Any leader who wishes to be great would do well to study Washington's life and personal views on leadership with a keen eye on the role humility played therein.

You may recall, from our discussion in this book's first chapter, how Washington's behavior, a paradigm of reluctant leadership, went beyond mere words in terms of humility and self-sacrifice. Both his actions and words reflected a sense of duty and selflessness that made him a beloved and respected figure. As the American Revolution came to a successful conclusion, Washington's leadership and military prowess were highly praised. Yet, when the opportunity arose for him to seize more power, he instead chose to relinquish it and retire to his plantation at Mount Vernon, emphasizing his wish for a peaceful private life after eight long years of war.

In 1787, when the Constitutional Convention concluded with a newly minted framework for a stronger federal government,

Washington was the unanimous choice to become the first President of the nascent United States of America. He expressed his reluctance to take on this role in a letter to Alexander Hamilton, asking, "Have I not done enough for my country?" His question echoed his genuine desire for respite and showed his lack of ambition for personal power. (Chernow, 2010.)

Washington's reluctant acceptance of the presidency embodied his view of leadership as a duty, not a quest for authority. He saw himself as a servant of the American people, ensuring the survival and growth of the young nation. His leadership style, grounded in humility and a deep sense of civic responsibility, resonates with our understanding of effective leadership. Indeed, leadership is not about wielding power but about guiding others towards shared goals.

Through the Gates of Humility

In addition to humility, for society to peacefully flourish, we harmony must emerge as a unifying social value. St. Paul, in his letter to the Church in Rome, wrote:

"Live in harmony with one another; do not be haughty, but associate with the lowly; never be conceited. Repay no one evil for evil, but take thought for what is noble in the sight of all. If possible, so far as it depends upon you, live peaceably with all. Do not be overcome by evil, but overcome evil with good."[18]

This was written during a time of extreme persecution of Christians in the Roman Empire. St. Paul, himself, was martyred in Rome under the Emperor Nero. No matter what happened to an individual in this vulnerable community, St. Paul wanted followers of Christ, in what was likely the most intense area of Christian persecution in the world at the time, to be known for living in harmony with one another, for being humble, for refraining from vengeance, for doing what is noble, and for living in peace.

To live a satisfying life, one should strive for harmony in their various considerations, rather than simply balance. Harmony involves aligning many considerations with a single unifying theme, rather than simply weighing one consideration against another. This is more complex than balance, but ultimately leads to a more fulfilling life.

For a satisfying and fulfilling life, one ought to align each consideration, each aspect of their life, with a single, unifying theme. This is how one may bring all the parts of his existence into harmony with each other.

I believe the greatest unifying virtue is charity. Charity is "willing the good of the other" with respect to each other individual we encounter. St. Paul had much to say about charity (some translations of his letters use the word "love,"). In his first letter to the church in Corinth, he wrote:

"If I speak in the tongues of men and of angels, but have not love, I am a noisy gong or a clanging cymbal. And if I have prophetic powers, and understand all mysteries and all knowledge, and if I have all faith, so as to remove mountains, but have not love, I am nothing. If I give away all I have, and if I deliver my body to be burned, but have not love, I gain nothing.

Love is patient and kind; love is not jealous or boastful; it is not arrogant or rude. Love does not insist on its own way; it is not irritable or resentful; it does not rejoice at wrong, but rejoices in the right. Love bears all things, believes all things, hopes all things, endures all things.

Love never ends; as for prophecies, they will pass away; as for tongues, they will cease; as for knowledge, it will pass away. For our knowledge is imperfect and our prophecy is imperfect; but when the perfect comes, the imperfect will pass away. When I was a child, I spoke like a child, I thought like a child, I reasoned like a child; when I became a man, I gave up childish ways. For now we see in a mirror dimly, but then face to face. Now I know in part; then I shall understand fully, even as I have been fully understood. **So faith, hope, love abide, these three; but the greatest of these is love.**" (emphasis mine)[19]

But What About ...

Leaders need to be virtuous and society needs to restore virtue. Some people may push back and try to challenge this idea, but it's really quite simple: just do the right thing. Nearly everyone knows what the right thing to do is. The difficulty is not understanding what the right thing to do *is*; it's *doing it* that's hard.

Many people have a functional conscience and can use that as a guide. For those who need more guidance, the Catechism of the Catholic Church can provide a clear path to a virtuous life.

Of course, no one will live a perfect life. We all need grace and forgiveness from time to time. In fact, genuinely forgiving others is required of every single real Christian.

Immediately after the verses in the Gospel of Matthew in which we find the Lord's Prayer, Jesus says, *in "red letter text,"* that our sins will not be forgiven if we do not forgive others.

"For if you forgive men their trespasses, your heavenly Father also will forgive you; but **if you do not forgive men their trespasses, neither will your Father forgive your trespasses."** Matthew 6:14–15 (emphasis mine)

Forgiving others is key to restoring our relationship with God. Holding grudges, bitterness, and resentment puts that relationship at risk. We must truly forgive by forgetting the wrongs others have done to us. This includes forgiving repeat offenders.

God wants us to live in love and peace with each other. By forgiving and forgetting, we can have a loving, peaceful life. A leader who strives to live by these principles and wants to be virtuous is worth following.

Memento Mori

"In all you do, remember the end of your life, and then you will never sin." Sirach 7:36

To live a virtuous life, always keep in mind that your actions will be judged by God. Reflect on your mortality and ask yourself if what you're doing is in line with God's will. Choose to forgive others and show mercy, as God has forgiven you. It won't be easy, but remember that true love for God means following His commandments.

Each day, consider the end of your life; and choose virtue. Choose God's will for your life, not simply what you desire.

This will be difficult, and may even seem impossible, but remember the rich young ruler in Matthew 19. If we are unwilling to sacrifice what is most precious to us for the love of God, which is keeping His commandments (John 14:21), then we do not really love God, will have no place with Him in Eternity, and are unworthy to be followed by anyone else.

Following this advice will lead you to a more virtuous life, and will make you more worthy of others' respect.

Embrace Virtue

It is clear that the lack of trust in public institutions and leaders is a major issue that needs to be addressed. This can only be achieved if we embrace virtue, humility, and charity, and reject moral relativism and intersectional (i.e., "identity") politics. By striving to live in harmony with one another, we can build a society that is more trustworthy and fulfilling.

So, what can you do to help improve leadership and embrace virtue in your own life? Start by examining your own behavior and striving to live with humility, selflessness, and patience. Forgive others, even repeat offenders, and seek to live a life of charity, willing the good of others. Remember that your actions will be judged by God and strive to align each aspect of your life with a single, unifying theme.

Finally, encourage those around you to embrace virtue and lead by example. The world needs more virtuous leaders and it starts with each of us taking action to become one. By following these principles, you can make a positive impact on your community and society as a whole.

KEY TAKEAWAYS

- Trust in public institutions and leaders is at an all-time low due to perceived lack of virtue and moral relativism in leadership.
- Virtuous leadership is needed to restore trust. Virtues such as humility, charity, and harmony are essential for effective leadership.
- Leaders should strive to align their actions with a single unifying theme, such as charity or humility, to bring harmony to their lives and their leadership.
- Forgiveness is a key aspect of virtuous leadership. Leaders should be willing to forgive others and seek forgiveness when necessary.
- Leaders should be aware of their mortality and the transient nature of their actions, striving to align their actions with God's will.
- The rejection of moral relativism and intersectional ideology is necessary for the restoration of virtuous leadership.

ACTION ITEMS

- Reflect on your own behavior and identify areas where you can practice more humility, selflessness, and patience.
- Practice forgiveness in your interactions with others, even with those who have wronged you repeatedly.
- Strive to align your actions with a single, unifying theme that reflects your core values and virtues.
- Regularly remind yourself of your mortality and the transient nature of your actions, using this as motivation to align your actions with virtuous principles.
- Consciously decide, as of this moment, to reject moral relativism and intersectionality. In the future, instead, choose to advocate for a return to virtue-based leadership, and lead by example.
- Explore the historical and philosophical foundations of virtue to gain a better understanding of why there are reasons to believe in the existence and value of virtue.

CHAPTER 13

Leadership by Design

Building on Foundational Leadership Traits

What qualities set truly exceptional leaders apart? While effective leadership takes many forms, research reveals several key traits consistently present in the most impactful leaders. In this chapter, we'll explore the top traits of influential leaders and how to develop them.

TRAITS OF POWERFUL LEADERS

Leadership is about inspiring others to reach their full potential and achieve shared goals. There are few traits that distinguish leaders from followers, but some of the most critical ones include intelligence, creativity, competency, decisiveness, social skills, and trustworthiness. These traits were first identified by Scottish philosopher Thomas Carlyle in his "Great Man" theory of leadership.

A more comprehensive list of traits associated with exceptional leaders includes being:

- Action-Oriented: Leaders who take decisive steps to advance their goals or those of their group.

- Charismatic: Inspiring and motivating others to give their best.

- Competent: Capable of efficiently and effectively getting the job done, or leading others to do so.

- Confident: Assertive without being overly aggressive.

- Courageously Resolved: Bravely committed to overcoming challenges for the good of their group.

- Creative: Possessing both personal creativity and the ability to inspire creative output from others.

- Decisive: Boldly making decisions without prolonged deliberation.

- Dynamic: Able to quickly and flexibly adapt to new circumstances.

- Intelligent: High I.Q. and strong social skills, capable of solving problems and navigating interpersonal relationships.

- Resilient: Tenacious commitment to completing their work.

- Responsible: Taking ownership of their work and not blaming others for setbacks.

- Self-assured: Confident in their value and competence, and trustworthy.

- Stalwart: Good control over their emotions, not prone to overreaction.

- Trustworthy: Committed to personal integrity, high ethical standards, and transparency.

- Understanding: Sensitive and respectful to the needs of others, with a genuine desire to see them succeed.

An effective leader must use these skills to competently organize collective efforts toward a common objective. Great leaders do this by setting an example, clearly sharing their vision, and pioneering new possibilities.

To develop these traits and become an effective leader, you can follow an easy-to-remember process called the **T-O-P** Method:

- **T**ake Inventory: Raise awareness of your resources and identify areas for improvement.

- **O**pt for Quick Wins: Focus on skill-building efforts that result in quick, positive outcomes.

- **P**ractice Until Ingrained: Reinforce and amplify the effects of the method by focusing on forming good habits.

> "Leadership is about inspiring others to reach their full potential and achieve shared goals."

Take Inventory

In the process of taking inventory, you'll assess which effective leadership traits are already a part of your behavior and which ones you need to work on. The goal is to make these traits instinctive, natural, and intuitive in your approach.

One method is to create two lists: one of traits you already possess and another of traits you'd like to develop. Then, prioritize the second list based on which traits come most naturally to you. This method is suitable for those who think critically and spend a lot of time in their heads.

Another approach, which is more heart-centered, involves a guided meditation. Here's how to do it:

Find a quiet place where you won't be disturbed for 10-20 minutes.

Sit on a cushion or chair, with your hands resting in your lap.

Close your eyes and take a few deep breaths. Imagine a line from the center of the earth through the top of your head. Focus your awareness on this line and bring your mind to the center of your body.

Allow each of the leadership traits to come to mind and ask yourself if you have a solid command of it. If the answer is "No," it's a trait you need to work on. If the answer is "Yes," it's a trait you already possess. If you're uncertain, assume you don't have a solid command of it.

Take note of any patterns, trends, or unexpected emotions that come up during the meditation.

End the meditation with a minute of restful calm, allowing everything to settle. Open your eyes.

Once you have a clear understanding of your strengths and weaknesses, it's time to make decisions about how you'll work on developing the necessary traits.

Opt for Quick Wins

The reward center of the human brain plays a significant role in driving our subconscious and heuristic thinking, which often goes unnoticed. This can be a double-edged sword as it can drive us towards bad habits and negative behaviors if not properly managed. Leaders must understand the importance of tapping into the reward center of their brain to sustain their motivation and drive towards their goals.

In order to develop effective leadership traits and make them a part of your character and behavioral portfolio, it's crucial to assess which traits will be the easiest for you to acquire, and prioritize their acquisition. By focusing on quick wins and consistently feeding the reward center of your brain, you'll be able to stay motivated and on track towards your goals.

First, start by focusing on the easy traits that come naturally to you. This will help you build momentum and establish a sense of accomplishment early on, which can help boost your confidence and keep you motivated. Once you've made progress with the easier traits, you can then move on to the harder, less attractive traits.

Understand, developing effective leadership traits is a continuous process, and not something that can be achieved overnight. Consistently focusing on quick wins and making small, incremental improvements, will help you gradually build up a strong portfolio of leadership traits over time.

The development of effective leadership traits requires a combination of self-awareness, self-reflection, and a commitment to continuous improvement. Prioritize the acquisition of the easiest traits first, and consistently feed the reward center of your brain. This way, you'll be able to stay motivated and make lasting changes to your character and behavior.

Practice Until Ingrained

How you practice each leadership trait is largely up to you. While working with a mentor or coach can provide guidance to faster, more efficient methods of growth, you can start your journey on your own by following these steps:

Meditate for 2-4 minutes on the trait you want to cultivate, visualizing examples of it.

Write out an affirmation that inspires you to embody that trait.

Brainstorm a daily task or habit to start taking action that exemplifies that trait in your life.

Reflect and refine at the end of the week.

While it is recommended to work with a holistic leadership mentor or coach, investing in consistent quick wins to incorporate more effective leadership traits into your leadership repertoire is key. Remember, as a leader, you should strive to inspire others to fulfill shared goals and guide them through a process of achieving them according to your vision.

Effective leaders leave a lasting impact through their followers who carry on the organization's work according to the leader's vision. Don't delegate leadership responsibilities to your team, as there is no substitute for your own leadership competence. Lead by example and stay focused on your vision to keep your team on track.

CULTIVATING YOUR LEADERSHIP TRAITS

With consistent practice, you can make these traits instinctive. Leadership is a journey, not a destination. By implementing the T-O-P model, you'll be well on your path to becoming an empowering leader.

Remember, the most influential leaders share certain traits like competence, confidence, and charisma, but, while strengths vary, exemplary leaders are most guided by their moral compass and zeal for their team's best interest.

You have an opportunity to leave a meaningful legacy by inspiring others. Cultivating your leadership abilities is an essential part of developing competence. Discover your gifts, get support, and practice deliberately.

You have the potential for greatness! The degree to which you fulfill that potential largely depends on your commitment to developing your competence. So, take these traits seriously if you want to claim your place among the leaders you look to for inspiration

KEY TAKEAWAYS

- Leadership is about inspiring others to reach their full potential and achieve shared goals. Exceptional leaders possess traits such as being action-oriented, charismatic, competent, confident, creative, decisive, dynamic, intelligent, resilient, responsible, self-assured, stalwart, trustworthy, and understanding.
- The T-O-P method (Take Inventory, Opt for Quick Wins, Practice Until Ingrained) is a useful approach to developing these leadership traits.
- Self-awareness and self-reflection are crucial in identifying one's strengths and areas for improvement.
- Quick wins, or focusing on traits that come naturally and can be developed easily, can help maintain motivation and drive towards goals.
- Developing effective leadership traits is a continuous process that requires consistent practice and commitment.

ACTION ITEMS

- Take inventory of your current leadership traits, identifying your strengths and areas for improvement.
- Prioritize the development of traits that come naturally to you for quick wins and to maintain motivation.
- Practice the traits you wish to develop until they become ingrained in your behavior.
- Use meditation and visualization to focus on the traits you wish to cultivate.
- Write out affirmations that inspire you to embody the traits you're working on.
- Brainstorm daily tasks or habits that exemplify the traits you're working to develop, and incorporate these into your routine.

CHAPTER 14

Embracing Disruption

Transforming Challenges into Opportunities

Encountering disruption is a challenge that leaders must face, as it is an inevitable and essential aspect of leadership. Therefore, developing the ability to constructively respond to disruption is a crucial leadership skill.

You may feel a sense of discomfort or even fear at the thought of disruption. But, instead of a typical tough love approach, this chapter aims to provide a more constructive and practical view of disruption. My goal is to help you understand and appreciate the value of disruption, so that you may even come to welcome it as an opportunity for positive change.

I'll illustrate this through my own personal experience. When I was 17, my family was struggling with persistent interpersonal and financial disruptions. At that time, I asked my grandmother if I could build an apartment in her unfinished basement. She generously agreed, even offering to pay for the materials needed for the project. With the help of my high school shop teacher, Mr. Baggett, and some boys from my shop class, I was able to complete the apartment.

Just in the nick of time, as my family was losing our home to foreclosure, I was able to move into the new apartment. Not only did I gain a stable place to live, I also created a dynamic of greater mutual support between my grandmother and myself.

Losing my childhood home was a traumatic experience, but it allowed me to build an even closer relationship with my grandmother and gave me the opportunity to live with her for six precious years.

After I moved out of that apartment, one of my younger sisters even lived there for a time, continuing the virtuous cycle of symbiosis I had established. For nearly a decade, the mutual support we were able to receive from and provide to my grandmother was a huge blessing to her and to us. Rather than seeing only the disruption of losing our home, I was able to perceive an opportunity to build something new that benefitted others I loved.

The ability to transform loss into opportunity is a powerful skill, requiring one to encounter disruption as more than just a setback. Disruptions can be difficult to encounter, but for leaders, practicing resilience in the face of disruption is an unavoidable and essential skill to learn.

In the rest of this chapter I will offer a constructive and practical approach to better understanding and even appreciating disruptions.

I know this is very hard, by the way! I used to view my life as a series of losses. Eventually, however, I learned to see opportunities in disruptions and encounter them in healthier ways. Instead of viewing disruptions only as challenges to overcome, great leaders see them as harbingers of opportunity. This shift in perspective helps leaders be the disruptors and embrace the assurance that what is torn down will be replaced with something better. With this new mindset, let's now dive into what disruption truly means and how leaders can encounter and respond to it effectively.

DISRUPTIONS AND DESTRUCTION: CLEARING UP MISCONCEPTIONS

In my work with executives and entrepreneurs, I've noticed that many people associate disruption with destruction. While destruction can certainly be disruptive, it's important to understand that not all disruptions lead to destruction. In fact, many creative solutions to persistent problems are born out of disruptions.

> **"Destruction leads to a very rough road, but it also breeds creation."**
> -- RED HOT CHILI PEPPERS

It's true that keeping things the same can be the best option in some cases, but this should not be seen as a depressing thought. Instead, it's an opportunity to embrace a more optimistic mindset and see disruptions as a chance to shake up the status quo and make improvements. This is because, in the absence of compelling reasons to believe that improvement is impossible, I believe that improvement is almost always possible.

The creative destruction process, also known as Schumpeter's gale, is a concept introduced by Austrian economist Joseph Schumpeter. He wrote that this process of industrial mutation continuously revolutionizes the economic structure from within, destroying old systems and creating new ones. In business and industry, change is inevitable and often involves old systems giving way to innovation. While destruction may be part of the process, so is creation.

With this new perspective on disruption, leaders can learn to encounter and respond to disruptions in a constructive way, pivoting themselves, their families, organizations, companies, and communities into more positive modes of operation.

ENCOUNTERING DISRUPTION

As a leader, encountering disruption is inevitable and a crucial skill to master. It's natural to feel intimidated by the word "disruption," but it's important to understand that it doesn't always have to be a negative thing. In fact, many creative solutions to persistent problems are born from disruption.

It's common for people to associate disruption with destruction, but this is not always the case. Disruptions can lead to new opportunities, allowing leaders to pivot their organizations, families, companies, and communities into more constructive modes of operation.

When facing disruption, it's important to approach it with an open mind, recognizing that opportunity is often close behind. If you're feeling uncertain, try taking a few minutes to simply observe your feelings and allow them to be there without evaluating them. Write down any feelings and their relation to specific aspects of the disruption, then make an effort to reframe these feelings in a positive light. With time, this mental habit will change the way you respond to disruption and help you see it as an opportunity for growth and improvement.

Great leaders not only encounter disruption constructively but also embrace it as a harbinger of opportunity. They understand that disruption is as much a force of creation as it is of destruction and that old things may pass away but they will be replaced with something better. With this assurance, great leaders can approach disruption with peace of mind.

Accepting and embracing disruption as a means of growth and improvement is a key aspect of being a great leader. By developing a positive mindset towards disruption, you can turn it into a source of creative solutions and opportunities.

KEY TAKEAWAYS

- Disruption is an inevitable part of leadership and can lead to positive outcomes if approached constructively.
- Disruption is often associated with destruction, but it can also lead to the creation of new and improved systems or solutions.
- The concept of "creative destruction," introduced by economist Joseph Schumpeter, suggests that industrial mutation continuously revolutionizes the economic structure from within, destroying old systems and creating new ones.
- Great leaders view disruption as an opportunity for growth and improvement, and they approach it with an open mind and a positive attitude.
- Developing a positive mindset towards disruption can turn it into a source of creative solutions and opportunities.

ACTION ITEMS

- Reflect on past disruptions in your life or career and consider how they led to positive changes or growth.
- Practice reframing your perspective on disruption, viewing it not as a threat but as an opportunity for improvement and innovation.
- Identify a current disruption in your life or work and brainstorm ways it could lead to positive outcomes or creative solutions.
- Develop a habit of observing your feelings towards disruption without judgment, and work on reframing these feelings in a positive light.
- Encourage your team or organization to embrace disruption as a chance for growth and improvement, and lead by example in responding to disruption with a positive and open-minded attitude.
- Continually remind yourself, and regularly remind your team, that while disruption may involve some destruction, it also opens the door for creation and innovation.

CHAPTER 15

Self-Trust

The Foundation of Confident Leadership

Confidence is a vital component of effective leadership, and it starts with self-trust. A leader who has lost confidence after a setback must work to regain it, as confidence is essential for inspiring trust in others. A leader who does not trust himself will find it difficult to earn the trust of others.

Comeback Confidence

When a leader fails to meet a duty or expectation, the first step is to understand the origin of the duty or expectation. If it was imposed by someone else and not truly accepted, the failure may simply reflect the leader being true to themselves. Additionally, it is important to consider whether the duty or expectation was reasonable. If it was unreasonable, then failing to meet it is a reasonable response.

In these cases, the problem is not with the leader's competence or character, and there is no reason to lose confidence.

It's also crucial to understand whether the failure was a one-off occurrence or part of a trend. If it was a fluke, and not part of a larger pattern, the leader should apologize and make amends if necessary, learn from the experience, and move on. If the failure was part of a trend, the leader should work on improving their character and competence, and then consider testing their leadership abilities again.

Reflecting on the failure, and considering what was learned from it, is also important. Keeping these reflections in a journal can be useful. Even when the failure was completely the leader's fault, it does not justify a loss of confidence if it was a one-time occurrence. Only if the failures become a trend should the leader reconsider their confidence.

Consider the example of Steve Jobs, who co-founded Apple and led the company to great success, but was ousted from Apple in 1985 after clashing with the board and CEO John Sculley. This was a major professional setback that likely shook Jobs' confidence.

However, he soon founded NeXT and Pixar, finding success again in both ventures. He also reconciled with Apple, which ended up acquiring NeXT in 1996. Jobs rejoined Apple during a period of decline and was able to lead an astonishing turnaround, launching revolutionary products like the iMac, iPod and iPhone.

Jobs remarkably regained confidence after his initial firing from Apple and evolved into an even more mature, focused leader during his second stint at Apple. He learned from early mistakes and centered himself by focusing on his passion for bringing innovative technology to consumers.

Competence Confidence

For some leaders, lacking confidence may stem from difficulty accepting they cannot be perfect. But imperfection is inevitable. The key is having a solid plan that accounts for missteps or changes. Here are tips for creating coherent plans as an imperfect leader:

- Be realistic about timeframes and budgets. Pad estimates to absorb surprises rather than clinging to unrealistic perfectionist goals.
- Build in margin by underpromising and overdelivering. Leave wiggle room in targets and expectations.
- Collaborate with your team to get broad input on viable plans. Two heads are better than one.
- Analyze past failures to anticipate potential pitfalls and missteps. How can you safeguard against these?
- Outline contingency plans for high-risk elements. Have a Plan B (and Plan C) ready.
- Leave room to refine plans as changes occur. Be flexible and adaptable.

With thoughtful preparation, imperfection doesn't have to prevent success. You can develop coherent plans that withstand reality's unavoidable messiness.

A leader who lacks clarity about their inner resources and resource network may struggle with confidence. Taking time to understand oneself, how one interacts with their team, and how they relate to their circumstances is essential.

Developing a greater awareness of connections with oneself, others, and the situation can help. Involving a coach, mentor, or teacher in this process can provide valuable insights. Once the leader has greater clarity about their resources, they will be better equipped to take steps towards their goals.

Character Confidence

A lack of confidence may also stem from a fear of taking reasonable risks. If this is the case, the leader should pause, gather their internal resources, and anchor themselves in their core values. If the leader's core values are no longer aligned with the plan of action or the core values of the organization, they may need to reconsider their role and refrain from taking action.

TUNING INTO CORE VALUES

When a leader's confidence wanes, it's often a signal to revisit and reflect on their core values. This is not merely an intellectual exercise but a deeply introspective one. Here are some steps to tune into one's core values:

1. Solitude and Silence: Allocate time for solitude where you can be free from distractions. Silence allows the inner voice to become more audible.

2. Deep Reflection: Ask yourself questions that probe the essence of your values. What principles are non-negotiable in your leadership? What virtues do you aspire to embody?

3. Consult Sacred Texts or Philosophical Works: Sometimes, wisdom from external sources like religious texts or philosophical works can offer valuable insights into your own values.

4. Dialogue with Trusted Advisors: Engage in conversations with mentors, coaches, or spiritual guides who understand your value system. They can provide an external perspective that you might not have considered.

5. Journaling: Write down your reflections and insights. This not only provides clarity but serves as a record you can revisit when faced with future challenges.

6. Alignment Check: Compare your actions and decisions against your core values. Are they in harmony? If not, what needs to change?

7. Prayer or Meditation: For those who are spiritually inclined, prayer or meditation can offer a deeper understanding and acceptance of one's core values.

8. By tuning into your core values, you not only gain clarity but also fortify your inner foundation, making you more resilient in the face of challenges and uncertainties.

If the leader is uncertain about their values, they should work to gain clarity. If they have clarity about their values and have learned from past failures, they should have confidence in their ability to make better choices in the future. If they lack this confidence, they may need to reflect on whether they have truly learned from past setbacks. All that can be done is to learn from the past and make the best decisions possible based on current awareness and available resources. This is all that others can reasonably expect.

> **"Confidence is essential for inspiring trust in others."**

BUILDING TRUST IN YOURSELF

Building trust in oneself starts with authenticity and accepting one's imperfections. A leader should never try to be someone they are not and should remain authentic and genuine. Setting reasonable goals, communicating those goals to the team, and getting buy-in from team members can also help build confidence. When goals are clear and everyone understands what they are working towards, collaboration is easier, and confidence is greater.

When it comes to setbacks and failures, it's crucial for a leader to remain confident and trust in themselves. The first step is to understand why the failure occurred. If it was due to an external factor, such as an unreasonable expectation or duty imposed by someone else, then there's no reason for the leader to lose confidence. If the failure was a fluke, and not part of a larger pattern, the leader should communicate with those affected, apologize if necessary, and move on. If the failure is part of a trend, it's important to reflect on what was learned and work on improving character and competence.

For leaders struggling with confidence, it's important to understand that being imperfect is okay. A wise leader will accept their imperfections and have a plan in place to achieve their goals. If a leader lacks clarity around their own inner resources and resource network, they should take time to reflect and consider involving a coach or mentor.

If a leader is too fragile to take reasonable risks, they should take a step back and anchor themselves in their core values. If a leader is questioning their values or hasn't learned from past setbacks, it's important to reflect on their core values and make the best decisions based on their current awareness and available resources.

Finally, it's essential for a leader to be kind and charitable to themselves. Within reasonable limits, they should give themselves permission to fail, learn, and grow. They should communicate with stakeholders that setbacks are a natural part of growth and improvement in any endeavor, and as long as they learn from their failures and make better decisions in the future, that is always good enough.

Building trust in oneself starts with authenticity, accepting imperfections, setting reasonable goals, and reflecting on failures. A leader should communicate with their team, anchor themselves in their core values, and be kind and charitable to themselves. With these steps in mind, a leader can build and maintain confidence in themselves, even in the face of setbacks and failures.

KEY TAKEAWAYS

- Confidence is a critical aspect of effective leadership, and it starts with trusting oneself. Leaders who trust themselves inspire trust in others.
- When a leader fails to meet an expectation, it's important to understand the origin of the expectation and whether it was reasonable. If the failure was a one-off occurrence, the leader should learn from the experience and move on. If it's part of a trend, the leader should work on improving their character and competence.
- Trusting oneself to be imperfect is a crucial aspect of leadership. Leaders should have a coherent plan for achieving their goals and understand that imperfection is okay.
- Building trust in oneself starts with authenticity, accepting imperfections, setting reasonable goals, and reflecting on failures. Leaders should communicate with their team, anchor themselves in their core values, and be kind and charitable to themselves.

ACTION ITEMS

- Reflect on past failures and consider what was learned from them. Keep a journal of these reflections to help understand patterns and areas for improvement.
- Take time to understand your inner resources and how you interact with your team and circumstances. Consider involving a coach, mentor, or teacher for valuable insights.
- If you're struggling with confidence due to a fear of taking reasonable risks, pause and anchor yourself in your core values. Reflect on whether your core values align with your plan of action or the core values of your organization.
- Work on building trust in yourself by being authentic, accepting your imperfections, and setting reasonable goals. Communicate these goals to your team and ensure everyone understands what they're working towards.
- If you're questioning your values or haven't learned from past setbacks, take time to reflect on your core values and make the best decisions based on your current awareness and available resources.
- Be kind and charitable to yourself. Give yourself permission to fail, learn, and grow, and communicate with stakeholders that setbacks are a natural part of growth and improvement.

CHAPTER 16

Mountain Tunnel, Canyon Bridge

The Art of Repairing Relationships

Leadership does not unfold in a vacuum; it is deeply enmeshed in the complex fabric of human relationships. The question, then, is not whether fractures will occur, but how one manages the often arduous task of mending them.

In some cases, relationships can suffer from neglect or drift apart over time, while in others, conflicts or hurt may arise and create barriers between individuals. Regardless of the cause, repairing relationships requires effort, communication, and time to rebuild trust and emotional intimacy.

It may come as a surprise how crucial it is to recognize the role of both healthy and unhealthy boundaries in the work of mending relational fractures, but that is precisely where we will begin this work.

BOUNDARIES

In earlier chapters, I have delved into the critical issue of boundaries—emotional, intellectual, and relational. Beyond what already has been said, it's worth noting that boundaries also play a crucial role in repairing relationships. These invisible lines are more than mere walls; they are finely tuned filters that preserve the integrity of the self, even as they engage the complexity of the outside world.

Unfortunately, even when one makes sincere and intentional efforts to repair relationships in an emotionally safe way, they may encounter pushback in the form of "boundaries." While it is important to acknowledge the need for and legitimacy of healthy boundaries, sometimes the supposed "boundaries" that keep us from repairing relationships are unhealthy, weaponized boundaries —barriers to emotional intimacy built on fear or even paranoia.

Healthy boundaries exist in the present, based on present conditions and the current state of individuals. Boundaries cannot be considered healthy if an individual is attached to the pain of the past or fear of the future.

Boundaries encountered during the process of reconciliation may not be based on the current state of individuals, but on past perceptions. In such cases, these boundaries may have evolved into emotional walls that isolate individuals and prevent them from seeing each other as they truly are.

To restore a relationship in which this has occurred, both individuals must make an intentional effort to tunnel through the emotional walls that separate them. Simply waiting for time to heal the relationship will not bring two people back together. Breaking through these emotional walls requires intentional effort and authentic forgiveness.

True forgiveness, offered freely and in love, can restore relationships and tear down the walls that separate individuals. Forgiveness is restorative and leads to reconciliation, or at least opens a path towards reconciliation through making amends.

Now, some boundaries might have been set up years ago, designed to protect us from past circumstances that no longer exist. These historical boundaries may have existed for a good reason, in the past, yet no longer be relevant to present realities. Leaders must be both willing and able to review and adjust these old demarcations (and gently inspire others to do the same), for they can easily become obsolete fortresses that ward off both harm and potential good.

> **"What matters most is making and maintaining a connection."**

BREAKING BARRIERS

Saint Augustine once wrote that forgiveness is the key that unlocks the door of resentment and the handcuffs of hatred. Indeed, the theological virtue of forgiveness is a cornerstone in the complex architecture of relational healing.

The healing and restoration of relationships requires an intentional effort to authentically forgive. This process takes time, focus, and personal strength, but the most important thing is for each person to consistently take steps towards each other. Repairing relationships may take weeks, months, or even years, but as long as both individuals remain focused on rebuilding the relationship and making constructive contributions, a connection will eventually be restored.

Connections are essential for emotional intimacy, safety, openness, and vulnerability. Our desire for emotional intimacy stems from our need for love, both to love others and to be loved by others. Drilling through the emotional barriers separating us from those who have hurt us or who we have hurt is an act of love and aligns with Jesus' call to love our enemies and those who have treated us badly.

While drilling through these emotional barriers may be hard work and may not guarantee a straight and efficient journey, what matters most is making and maintaining a connection. The connection can always be improved over time. Repairing relationships and overcoming emotional barriers is fulfilling work for all of us as human beings.

BUILDING BRIDGES

Sometimes, what's needed to repair a relationship isn't drilling through an emotional mountain range, but building a bridge to cross a divide of indifference that has pushed people apart. The problem isn't necessarily a mountain of hurt, but a canyon of neglect that separates individuals.

The ultimate goal is to make a connection, regardless of its imperfections.

Relationships often fall apart due to neglect. Sometimes we consciously push away from others to protect ourselves or because we simply don't enjoy their company. Other times, we unintentionally drift apart because we prioritize other relationships or activities. As time passes, the connection between individuals erodes, and a void opens up where shared experiences would have been. Filling in these gaps requires intentional effort, communication, and time to restore understanding and trust.

To repair a relationship with someone who has drifted apart, making a new connection is crucial. This can involve catching up and sharing experiences and feelings to fill in the gaps in each person's memories and impressions. Although these conversations will always be imperfect, they're still better than no connection at all. Emotional bridges can link individuals together and enough of them can reconnect them in meaningful ways, allowing emotional intimacy to return to the relationship.

Building bridges requires effort, communication, and time, but the investment both individuals make in this work will largely determine the strength and stability of the emotional bridges between them. By making a conscious effort to prevent deep, wide canyons from forming in the first place, individuals can strengthen their relationships and foster a love that can flourish even when they've drifted apart.

The courage to close the gap is not unlike the courage shown by martyrs, for it has its power in the vulnerability required to achieve a goal greater than one's immediate comfort. Spanning a chasm — whether its genesis was in neglect or caustic conflict — requires so much more than good intentions. Action is absolutely necessary. The courage to act must arise and be sustained through both triumph and defeat, for those attempting such a sometimes-Herculean feat will surely experience both on their path to ultimate victory.

Repairing relationships is about fostering a connection, not necessarily having a perfect one. Relationship repair is a continuous process, not a singular event. Each investment, each act of kindness or understanding, adds another plank to the bridge. It is a labor of love, one that should be undertaken with both optimism and pragmatism.

The work of repairing relationships is rarely accomplished without setbacks and other flaws in execution, but even an imperfect connection can be valuable. In the words of Pope Francis, "We are all frail; everyone is frail." Yet it is in our frailty that our humanness is laid bare, offering a rich soil in which seeds of resilience and grace can grow. The effort and time invested in building emotional bridges can restore understanding and trust, leading to a return of emotional intimacy in the relationship.

KEY TAKEAWAYS

- Repairing relationships is a crucial aspect of leadership, requiring effort, communication, and time to rebuild trust and emotional intimacy.
- Healthy boundaries are important in relationships, but they can become unhealthy emotional walls if they're based on past perceptions or fears about the future.
- True forgiveness, offered freely and in love, can restore relationships and tear down the walls that separate individuals.
- The process of repairing relationships requires consistent steps towards each other, focusing on rebuilding the relationship and making constructive contributions.
- Sometimes, repairing a relationship involves building a bridge to cross a divide of indifference or neglect, rather than drilling through an emotional mountain range.
- The goal of repairing relationships is to make a connection, not necessarily to have a perfect one. The effort and time invested in building emotional bridges can restore understanding and trust.

ACTION ITEMS

- Reflect on your relationships and identify any that may have been neglected or damaged. Consider what steps you can take to repair these relationships.
- Evaluate the boundaries in your relationships. Are they healthy and based on present conditions, or have they become unhealthy emotional walls based on past perceptions or fears about the future?
- Practice forgiveness in your relationships, both in offering it to others and accepting it from them. Remember that forgiveness is restorative and can open a path towards reconciliation.
- Make a consistent effort to rebuild damaged relationships, even if the process takes time. Keep the focus on making constructive contributions and restoring the connection.
- If a relationship has drifted apart due to neglect, make an effort to build a bridge across the divide. This could involve catching up, sharing experiences, and filling in the gaps in each other's memories and impressions.
- Invest time and effort in preventing deep divides from forming in your relationships in the first place. This can strengthen your relationships and foster a love that lasts.

CHAPTER 17

The Power of Authentic Leadership

Building Trust and Psychological Safety

Effective leadership hinges on trust, which essentially is a willingness to be vulnerable to others' actions because we believe in their good intentions and we accept on faith their intentions to treat us well. In most cases, trust arises as the result of nurturing over time, rather than being a spontaneously existing component of a relationship. Over time, nurturing creates a sense of psychological safety.

Psychological safety directly influences trust, because when human beings feel a strong sense of connection, and especially belonging, they are far more easily able to relax and to trust. "Psychological safety" isn't just a corporate buzzword or a term entering our discourse because it's a pop psychology fad. Psychological safety is a genuine emotional state in which an individual feels secure enough to authentically share deep fears, beliefs, and hopes.

To be effective, leaders need to ask, "How can I inspire trust by nurturing others, thereby cultivating in them a state of psychological safety?"

"Being authentic is one of the fastest ways to create psychological safety in the workplace.

Psychological safety is the sense that we can share our feelings, beliefs, and experiences openly with others at work without fear of reprimand, losing status, or punishment.

Studies on psychological safety conducted in collaboration between Google and the Massachusetts Institute of Technology (MIT) found it to be one of the most important factors in creating successful teams and thus high performing, innovative organizations.

This insight is the result of almost 30 years of research by Amy Edmondson. Psychological safety supports moderate risk taking, speaking your mind, creativity, and most importantly trust. In my work with teams and senior leaders, I assess the psychological safety of the individual leader, the team and the culture first.

Before we try to be courageous in our interactions with others, we need the courage to understand ourselves and what's important to us."[20]

People frequently use the phrase "being authentic" in modern workplaces, yet the term carries substantial weight. Authenticity requires you to reconcile a dialectic tension between your inner world—your values, beliefs, and individual experiences—and an outer world comprising societal norms, organizational culture, and external expectations. This reconciliation allows you to remain the same person in private and public settings, fostering an atmosphere of psychological safety.

As Brené Brown writes, "Courage starts with showing up and letting ourselves be seen." In other words, leaders must first have the courage to examine their values and aspirations before they can inspire courage in their teams.

For great leaders, creating psychological safety is a high priority, whether they're creating it for themselves or their followers. As a leader, you are a role model and must cultivate trustworthiness by modeling psychological safety for those you lead. This applies not only to you but also to your entire tribe—those you're leading, in whatever context that leadership may be manifest.

Trustworthiness isn't merely a beneficial trait; it's a virtue. In this broader context, trustworthiness transcends the realm of secular leadership skills to become an act of faith and moral integrity, rounding out and grounding your leadership approach.

MODELING PSYCHOLOGICAL SAFETY

As a leader, whether you like it or not, you will be looked to as a role model. To cultivate trustworthiness, you must model the psychological safety you hope to create in your team's environment.

> **"The tribe supports the individual, just as the individual sustains the tribe."**

If you've experienced past traumas or setbacks, creating a safe environment can become a challenge. This book is for those leaders who have faced setbacks that have compromised their ability to lead, but who still want—or need—to lead. Such setbacks often involve traumatic losses. If you're feeling uncertain about your ability to create psychological safety, don't worry. Your commitment to resilient leadership, particularly when dealing with life's challenges, showcases your fortitude. You can cultivate psychological safety within yourself and others by surrounding yourself with people who are also committed to being intentional about it.

Leaders act as an organization's tuning fork; their vibrational energy sets the tone for everyone else. When you model psychological safety in your behavior, you empower others to do the same. Remember the old adage: "The tribe supports the individual, just as the individual sustains the tribe." This is why leaders are responsible for the vibe of their tribe.

I work with my clients to make authentic connections, enhance psychological safety, and cultivate trustworthiness in themselves and their organization. Together, we weave a psychological safety net.

This involves the practice of up to 32 different behavioral exercises. Due to the space constraints, these exercises are included in this book's **Appendix II: "Weaving the Psychological Safety Net."**

PRACTICE WEAVING THE NET

I recommend, on a piece of paper, making a list equal to the number of days in this month (get creative with February). Go through the exercises in Appendix II, and write down, in order of personal priority, each one, assigning them all to a numerical day of the month. (Feel free to leave out any that don't speak to you.)

You might keep the same list from month to month, or you might change things up from one month to the next as your personal priorities change in response to your growth as a leader.

In any event, take one day each month to focus on one of these exercises. Make it the object of your meditations. Write it on your whiteboard, or set a mindful alert on your phone, write it on a sticky note, or do something else that will remind you to spend time integrating the exercise into your feelings, attitudes, thoughts, words, and actions.

Change takes time, especially when past trauma is involved. However, by taking small steps, you can make progress and build a strong connection.

KEY TAKEAWAYS

- Trust is a willingness to be vulnerable to others' actions because we believe in their good intentions and we accept on faith their intentions to treat us well. Trust arises as the result of nurturing over time, creating psychological safety.
- Psychological safety is the emotional state where one can share feelings, beliefs, and experiences openly without fear of reprimand or loss of status. It is a cornerstone for successful teams and high-performing organizations.
- Leaders are the tuning forks of an organization, setting the tone for psychological safety and trustworthiness. They must model the psychological safety they wish to instill.
- Trustworthiness is not merely a beneficial trait but a virtue, transcending secular leadership skills to become an act of faith and moral integrity.
- Leaders can cultivate psychological safety and trustworthiness within themselves and their teams through intentional practices, as outlined in Appendix II.

ACTION ITEMS

- Reflect on your own experiences and understand how they might be affecting your ability to create psychological safety and cultivate trustworthiness.
- Surround yourself with individuals who are also committed to intentional practices that enhance psychological safety and trustworthiness.
- Review the exercises in Appendix II and prioritize them based on your personal and leadership needs. Assign each exercise to a day of the month for focused meditation and practice.
- Utilize reminders, such as writing the exercise of the day on a whiteboard or setting a mindful alert, to integrate these practices into your daily life.
- Be patient with yourself. Change takes time, especially when past trauma is involved. By taking small steps, you can make progress and build a strong connection.

PART TWO

Navigating the Storm

CHAPTER 18

Leading with Awareness

The Path of Mindful Resilience

Welcome to a different kind of exploration of the heart of mindful leadership. This chapter aims to explore the concept of mindfulness and its profound impact on leadership. We will delve into its definition, its spiritual roots, its practical applications, and much more.

Mindfulness is "paying attention to the present moment without judgment or criticism."[21] If you've been wondering what all the fuss is about, now, at least, you know what mindfulness is.

"We are created in the image of God, who is the infinite epitome of mindfulness. If mindfulness is awareness of the present moment, God is the present moment. He defined himself as 'I am who am.' God sees all as a present moment, and it is our goal to see as he sees. We will never see all as he does, but we can see what we see with the light of the present moment."[22]

A great part of practicing wisdom is actively trusting God with your life's circumstances. This is not passive surrender but active surrender — dynamic, conscious releasing of each present moment to God by intentionally choosing to trust Him. When one does this, his focus shifts from reaction to intentional permission, from judgment to consideration, from speaking to listening, and from evaluation to observation.

It is crucial, then, that a leader regularly and frequently practice mindfulness to increase his awareness of what is actually present, within and without. Unless we observe, without evaluating, what is, we cannot respond appropriately to it, in light of what ought to be. This act of surrender not only deepens our spiritual life but also serves as a cornerstone for mindful leadership, allowing us to approach challenges with a balanced and focused mind.

Building on the idea of mindfulness, it's important to recognize that our internal state plays a significant role in our leadership capabilities. You are solely responsible for how you experience and respond to everything you encounter in your life. At all times, you are free to choose to experience good, positivity, healthiness, and happiness. Likewise, you are free to choose to experience badness, negativity, toxicity, and misery. Whatever you you encounter, your experience will come from within you. As Jimi Hendrix said, "It all has to come from the inside." The choice to experience those things which will make you a better leader have to come from inside.

Whatever happens to you, whatever events or people you encounter—no matter how evil they are—cannot defile your spirit. Only what you choose to allow to take root within you can defile you. Only the evil you allow in can defile you, and whatever you have in abundance within your heart is what will come out of your mouth.

In the Gospel According to St. Mark, Jesus put it this way:

"And [Jesus] said, 'What comes out of a man is what defiles a man. For from within, out of the heart of man, come evil thoughts, fornication, theft, murder, adultery, coveting, wickedness, deceit, licentiousness, envy, slander, pride, foolishness. All these evil things come from within, and they defile a man.'"[23]

In the Gospel According to St. Luke, Jesus said:

"The good man out of the good treasure of his heart produces good, and the evil man out of his evil treasure produces evil; for **out of the abundance of the heart his mouth speaks.**" (emphasis mine)[24]

So, Observe. Allow. Be open. Notice. Acknowledge.

None of these things require judgment or evaluation from you — certainly not condemnation. Withhold judgment. Refrain from condemnation or even evaluation. Simply observe.

"Why," one might ask, "would I practice such a principle?"

Peace. The answer to that question is: peace. To find inner peace, calm at the center of life's storms, cultivating the skill of observation without evaluation enhances your capacity to be present in your circumstances, yet unperturbed by them.

"We have only the gentlest influence over our circumstances."

In each passing moment, we have only the gentlest influence over our circumstances. God is in control of everything, and He is trustworthy. In most moments of our lives, we need not evaluate but observe, we need not speak (inwardly or to others) but listen, we need not react but allow. By embracing this mindset, we can better navigate the complexities of our day-to-day lives, making each moment an opportunity for mindful leadership.

As you go through the rest of your day, see whether you can make an effort to simply observe, rather than evaluate, your circumstances. At the end of the day, make time to consider how this effort influenced your interactions with others and shaped your internal perceptions. Even in this reflective moment, however, refrain from evaluation; simply observe.

Each day that you do this, you will expand your meta-conscious capacity, and find yourself closer to clarity and inner peace.

EXPANDING MIND: FOCUSING YOUR MINDFUL PRACTICE

Where is your focus? Are you drawn to the darker side of things or the lighter side?

I used to focus on what I considered 'realistic' perspectives, believing them to be true. People would tell me to look on the bright side. I would resist this, because I felt that was arbitrarily choosing to be "positive," rather than objective.

Trying to be completely objective is, at best, futile and, at worst, arrogant, because of the finite qualities of our minds, we have been given the gift of focus.

Focus can be dominated by overwhelming thoughts and emotions. If, however, we develop awareness and consciousness that expands our capacity to make better choices about our inner life, it can be directed according to our will.

Our emotions are guided by our cravings, instincts, love, and fears. Our emotions influence or determine our thoughts. Our thoughts determine our words and actions. Our words and actions affect our circumstances.

All of these things are connected — inextricably intertwined. Are you cultivating meta-conscious awareness, a capacity to allow a thought to come to your mind without disturbing your emotions or dominating your focus? if not you may frequently feel completely overwhelmed by your cravings, instincts, fears, or loves.

For most of my life, I have been overwhelmed by these things. Now, however, I feel my meta-consciousness expanding (little by little) as I continue to practice mindful meditation; pray and draw closer to God; and, in a conscientious way, treat others as I would like to be treated.

Now, I realize that what I considered being realistic was really just focusing on the "how," the mechanics of choices and decisions. I was focused on the method, not the goal or object of my love. I had that focus, ironically, because I craved stability and safety, I feared loss, I lost the instinctive ability to separate ally from enemy and to deeply trust those who genuinely love me.

As my awareness expands, little by little, I am recovering a precious gift — the gift of focus. I am recovering the ability to see that positive and negative are equally real. When we do the internal work of personal growth, we gain (or can regain) the ability can choose where to place our focus. With this regained focus, we are better positioned to make conscious choices about our leadership style and the spaces—both literal and metaphorical—where we choose to 'sit' in our lives.

Both perspectives reflect reality. I am coming to believe that we find more peace, attract healthier relationships, and have better opportunities, when we choose to focus on love, not fear; the objects of your deepest desires, not the methods for obtaining them; and simply trusting God to move in your life and bring you closer to Him, rather than trying to be or do what you (or others) think you should.

MASTER'S MIND: WHERE YOU SIT

"Where do you stand," is a common challenge, echoing the idiom to "stand one's ground." We are called to "stand" for something — our principles, values, faith, etc. We say we are standing on our beliefs, our confidence in those ideas we hold to be true, and the like.

However, the place where you choose to sit holds equal significance. Sitting, in meditation, is active and powerful. Sitting and turning our focus inward offers us the opportunity to enter the Eternal Now, open our hearts and minds to harmony with everyone and all creation, and accept the present as we find it, without evaluation or judgment.

We need not spend all our time in meditation, or suspend all judgment forever. We need only do that which is necessary, right here and now, and that is to simply sit and breathe and be.

Leaders tend to be seated in places of power. Kings occupy thrones; the president sits at his desk in the Oval Office, where all recognize his authority; hosts (or honored guests) sit at the head of the table; and pilots, captains, and drivers take their seat at their vehicles' controls. Where (and how) one sits signifies their capacity to command a situation.

In meditation, we focus on being awake and alert. So, too, in leadership, we do not want to be said to be distracted or asleep at the wheel. The skills and traits we cultivate in meditation are essential for leaders, because they prepare our minds and hearts to receive each moment, accept it, observe it, and then choose whether and how to respond. This is how a mature leader behaves; he is not reactive or hard-charging.

The mature leader commands from his Singular Seat, secure in his authority and strength. This isn't mere arrogance; it's a genuine belief in your own abilities and trustworthiness. This is absolute confidence.

"Please, be seated;" "take your seat;" or "come, sit with us" are all invitations to accept one's place or role in a certain context. In the context of your own life — in both a literal, meditative way and a figurative, mindset way — I invite you to take your seat.

Assume command of your life. Sit in stillness and relax just enough to ease into a comfortable, quiet moment of confident control over your breath and your mind. Focus, but only enough to remain seated, undistracted by your surroundings or potential interruptions.

This is the doorway to the Eternal Now. This is confidence in practice. There is no "fake it 'till you make it" bullshit, here. There is no arrogant swagger. There is no imposter syndrome. There is no uncertainty. In this moment, there's no unmet need, incomplete task, or urgent issue demanding your attention.

You have turned off Notifications on Life, itself.

Here, you are seated, and you are in command. Abide in this place a while. Return as frequently as you need to. This place is always here, inside you. Enter the Eternal Now until it becomes the only state of being there is in your awareness, for in that moment, you will shed duality of mind and see things as they are.

That is the perspective of a leader, and, by daily meditating in this way, each day, we get a little closer to making it our own.

KEY TAKEAWAYS

- Mindfulness is paying attention to the present moment without judgment or criticism. It is a crucial tool for leaders to create psychological safety and trust within their teams.
- Leaders are responsible for their own experiences and responses to everything they encounter in life. They have the choice to experience positivity, healthiness, and happiness or negativity, toxicity, and misery.
- Practicing mindfulness can help leaders expand their meta-consciousness, allowing them to make better choices about their inner life and not be overwhelmed by their cravings, instincts, fears, or loves.
- The practice of mindful meditation can help leaders recover the gift of focus, allowing them to choose where to place their focus and see that positive and negative are equally real.
- The act of sitting in meditation is a powerful tool for leaders. It signifies their capacity to command a situation and prepares their minds and hearts to receive each moment, accept it, observe it, and then choose whether and how to respond.

ACTION ITEMS

- Practice mindfulness daily, paying attention to the present moment without judgment or criticism.
- Reflect on your own experiences and responses to everything you encounter in life. Make a conscious choice to experience positivity, healthiness, and happiness.
- Use mindful meditation to enhance your awareness and consciousness. This practice will help you make more informed choices about your emotional well-being.
- Concentrate on love over fear, and on your ultimate goals rather than the means to achieve them; and simply trusting God to move in your life and bring you closer to Him, rather than trying to be or do what you (or others) think you should.
- Spend time in meditation, focusing on being awake and alert. Assume command of your life and sit in stillness, easing into a comfortable, quiet moment of confident control over your breath and your mind.

CHAPTER 19

Nurturing the Leader's Soul

A Journey Within

In this chapter, we delve into an often-overlooked but crucial aspect of leadership: the interior life, or "inner journey" of a leader. As leaders, one's external actions often take precedence, or, at least, dominate our focus. The inner journey, however, is what fuels and sustains us. Therefore, it deserves special attention, and never should be neglected. In this chapter, we'll explore some foundational theological understandings that ought to guide a leader's inner life, drawing from sacred texts and papal wisdom. I'll also introduce you to an 'Interior Life Survival Kit,' I've developed—a set of spiritual and practical tools designed to navigate the complexities within.

From the role of discernment to the importance of mentors and even the food that nourishes our bodies, this chapter serves as a comprehensive starting point for cultivating an inner life that not only withstands the challenges of leadership but thrives in spite of them.

Having established the importance of the interior life in leadership, let's delve into what this means on a spiritual level.

The Imperative of the Interior Life in Leadership

A leader's inner journey should be a quest to find God in all things. This is a large pill to swallow for secular humanists or those for whom religion is more cultural artifact than a life of spiritual devotion. Based on both extensive observation and personal experience, however, I believe a life of prayer and the practice of living in the presence of God is the best way to ensure one can survive any setback and reclaim calm amid any crisis. When a leader engages in frequent and intimate dialogues with their Creator, focusing intentionally on the quality of their internal prayer life rather than merely on external actions, they open a conduit to supernatural resilience, hope, faith, and charity. In this state of spiritual alignment, even their actions transform into a form of prayer. Now that we've explored the spiritual imperatives of leadership, let's examine the theological foundations that can guide a leader's inner journey.

Theological Foundations and Practical Implications

In the Gospel According to St. John, we find Jesus teaching his disciples, "without me you can do nothing" (cf. Jn 15:5). This teaching underscores the importance of spiritual grounding in leadership. Leaders often feel the weight of the world on their shoulders, believing that outcomes rest solely on their efforts. However, this scriptural wisdom reminds us that our strength and wisdom come from a higher source. In practical terms, this could mean starting your day with prayer or meditation, seeking divine guidance in decision-making, or even consulting spiritual mentors when faced with ethical dilemmas.

In his apostolic letter, *Novo Millennio Ineunte*, St. John Paul II wrote, "It is prayer which roots us in this truth. It constantly reminds us of the primacy of Christ and, in union with him, the primacy of the interior life and of holiness." St. John Paul II's words serve as a reminder that a leader's effectiveness is deeply rooted in their interior life. It's not enough to be skilled in management techniques or strategic thinking; a leader must also cultivate an inner sanctum of prayer and holiness. This could manifest in the workplace as ethical leadership, a commitment to social justice, or fostering a culture of respect and dignity for all.

In his first encyclical *Deus caritas est*, Pope Benedict XVI echoed Jesus's teaching, reminding us that one "cannot always give, he must also receive." Pope Benedict XVI's insight is particularly relevant for leaders who find themselves constantly in the role of the giver— of time, energy, and resources. The Pope reminds us that to give effectively, one must also be open to receiving. In a leadership context, this could mean being open to feedback, delegating tasks to empower team members, or taking time for self-care and spiritual renewal.

Additionally, in *Deus caritas est*, Pope Benedict XVI emphasized the necessity of experiencing the truth, that God is Love, in one's interior life. Our prayer life "allows God to work," he writes, for He is "the only One who can make the world both good and happy." This teaching underscores the transformative power of a leader's interior life. When we allow God to work through our prayer life, we open ourselves to divine wisdom and guidance that can profoundly influence our leadership. This is not merely a passive act but an active collaboration with the Divine. It means that our decisions, actions, and interactions with others can be imbued with a higher purpose and ethical grounding. In this way, leadership becomes not just a role, but a vocation that contributes to making the world 'both good and happy.

The work leaders do is inherently draining. The work, itself, is mentally, physically, and spiritually exhausting, even though, at times, it can be exhilarating and liberating. Leaders work in service of others, championing ideals, goals, and shared values, especially when others are confused, misguided, or unmotivated. With a solid theological foundation in place, let's turn our attention to the practical tools and strategies that can sustain a leader's soul.

Sustaining the Leader's Soul: Tools and Strategies

Because great leaders constantly pour themselves into others, they need to be refilled by their Source. They need to be replenished spiritually, emotionally, and physically by their Creator. Going on a vacation or even taking a sabbatical is often insufficient for a leader to deeply recharge. (Sometimes, after a vacation, I feel like I need a vacation.)

> **"Because great leaders constantly pour themselves into others, they need to be refilled by their Source."**

Leaders must tend their inner lives like forest rangers. They must constantly blaze the trails on which they allow others to walk. They need to work to regularly do the work of ensuring their inner life is free of psychological pitfalls and spiritual hazards.

For this reason, great leaders allocate necessary resources to go on retreats, engage mentors and coaches, and other necessities for cultivating a rich interior life. The remainder of this chapter describes what I call the "Interior Life Survival Kit."

These are tools you already have—whether or not you realize it, right now. Consider this a briefing on how to effectively deploy them in your life. Having discussed the tools for sustaining a leader's soul, let's delve into the specifics of the "Interior Life Survival Kit" that every leader should possess.

INTERIOR LIFE SURVIVAL KIT

Leaders serious about surviving setbacks and defending their inner calm need a specific set of tools for safely and effectively pioneering their interior life. Like a Spanish Conquistador on a quest for the Fountain of Youth, your journey will take you through metaphorical jungles and swamps, over mountains and rivers, and into territory occupied by others whose avatars will be friendly, wary, hostile, or some combination of dispositions.

The Source that has sent you on this expedition, and will replenish you each time you return to Him, has provided you with all the tools you need to succeed on the journey into your interior life.

I am no longer of the opinion that, "God helps those who help themselves;" I've seen too many miracles to hold to such a cynical view.

Remember the words of Christ: "without me you can do nothing." St. Paul echoed this when he wrote, in his letter to the Church at Philippi, "I can do all things through Christ, who strengthens me." We are the doers; Christ is the Source and the Summit of all we are and do.

I say all this to say, the following tools are means, not ends. So, don't get too hung up on them. Also, keep in mind that these are not the only tools at your disposal; they're just the ones I consider absolutely essential.

A Sharp Knife

My friend, Joe Maynard founded Primitive Grind™ and crafts beautiful knives, each of which tell a beautiful story through their materials and craftsmanship. Joe has invested in a mobile forge he uses to visit trade shows and to surprise worthy individuals with an opportunity to craft a knife with him, without having to come to his workshop. Joe is a decorated veteran, who flew helicopters in Afghanistan and other theaters of conflict, and an amazing human being.

Joe was also on the reality TV show, Naked and Afraid. He's a natural storyteller and has a mind as sharp as the knives he creates. While I've carried a pocket knife for much of my life, until I met Joe, I had never had a handcrafted knife. Through Joe, I've come to have a better understanding of, and place a higher value on having a good knife.

After observing Joe's meticulous craftsmanship in knife-making, I can't help but draw parallels to the craftsmanship required in leadership. Just as Joe carefully selects the best materials, tempers the steel, and hones the blade to perfection, so too must a leader carefully cultivate their interior life. The steel is akin to our soul, requiring constant tempering through prayer and reflection. The honing process is like the ongoing work of self-examination and spiritual mentorship, sharpening our focus and purpose. And just as a well-crafted knife is both beautiful and functional, a well-cultivated interior life makes us not only effective leaders but also individuals of depth and substance.

Your Interior Life Survival Kit also contains a sharp knife, called Discernment. Although, the spiritual practice of discernment—especially Ignatian Discernment—are slightly outside the scope of this book's focus, I encourage you to explore that topic. Regarding discernment, I want to call your attention to its essential use as a separator.

Sharpen this tool, care for it, and never hesitate to use it. When presented with a new opportunity or task, your awareness should respond, like a muscle memory, by reaching for Discernment. Discerning whether something presented to your awareness is essential to you and responding appropriately will ensure you always have enough time for the things that matter most.

Guide, Granola, and Game plan

Your Interior Life Survival Kit also has a subset of tools crafted to work together to care for your mind, body, and spirit—the Three 'Gs:' Guide, Granola, and Game plan.

The 'Guide' is a coach + mentor. There are people in your life who have knowledge and wisdom you need to proficiently navigate the obstacles you face. Neglect these guides at your peril. They may be priests, psychologists, psychiatrists, coaches, mentors, teachers, elderly family members, or friends who have gracefully endured great suffering. To illustrate, consider the story of Steve Jobs and his mentor, Mike Markkula. Markkula provided Jobs not only with essential business advice but also life guidance, exemplifying the indispensable role of a 'Guide' in your Interior Life Survival Kit.

The Granola is... well, exactly that—it's just granola. Okay, well, maybe it's not just granola. It's healthy food. 'Granola' is a catch-all term for healthy eating. 'Garbage in, garbage out,' is as true for the body as it is for the mind. Cultivating a rich interior life is far more difficult when one is constantly distracted by physical ailments resulting from a poor diet. In the case of Steve Jobs, his specific diet, often consisting of fruits and smoothies, serves as a real-world example of the 'Granola' in action.

'Game plans,' while essential, are inherently flexible and ought to be carefully selected with your Guides. Notice, I said, 'with your Guides,' not, 'by your Guides,' and certainly not, 'for your Guides' or 'without your Guides.' You need a carefully crafted strategy, tactical approach, and plan of action. Having an outside view in both creating and implementing your game plan is essential to your success. Jobs' ability to pivot and adapt Apple's strategy over the years showcases the importance of a flexible 'Game plan.' He didn't achieve his monumental success alone; he had his guides, his health regimen, and a flexible strategy, all of which contributed to his resilience and effectiveness.

Talisman

Of all the tools in your Interior Life Survival Kit, the Talisman is among the most powerful and the most dangerous. The power comes from its inherent qualities. The danger arises from misunderstanding those qualities.

Your talisman will be unique to you (even if it's the same sort of thing other leaders have chosen as their talisman); and, properly employed, your talisman will point you to your Source. Like flint and tinder, your talisman can ignite a spark that can quickly become either a source of life-giving energy or a disastrous, all-consuming inferno.

To elucidate this point, consider the example of Mother Teresa. She carried a crucifix and a rosary, her talismans, wherever she went. These were not mere accessories but powerful symbols that connected her to her Source. They reminded her of her mission and the divine strength she could tap into. Her use of these talismans was deeply reverential and aligned with their inherent spiritual qualities, serving as a source of life-giving energy rather than a superstitious charm.

The benefit (or danger) of the Talisman is inextricably intertwined with one's use of it. The difference between blessing or curse is whether or not one's use of the Talisman is well-informed and appropriate to its inherent qualities. Here, again, one ought to employ Discernment and utilize his Talisman as prudence dictates.

Journal

Few great explorers failed to keep a record of their expeditions. I can't think of many. A record of your inner journey is an essential tool in your Interior Life Survival Kit.

Not only will a journal help you recall where you started, how far you have come, and all that has happened along the way, it can also serve as a useful, even instructive map of the topography of a human life. To illustrate the transformative power of journaling, consider the poignant example of Anne Frank. While hiding from the Nazis, she documented her experiences, thoughts, and emotions. Her journal not only served as a personal outlet but also as a historical record that has educated and inspired millions. Like Anne, keeping a journal can help you navigate the complexities of your inner life, serving as both a personal and potentially communal guide.

While each person's inner journey is unique, a canyon is a canyon and a valley is a valley, a mountain is a mountain and a river is a river. Identifying both types of topographical features and ways of constructively navigating them is useful for individual leaders and those whose experiences are similar.

Trinkets

On your journey into your inner life, you will encounter representations of other people in a variety of ways. These representations, or 'avatars,' are natives of your inner life, projected reflections of yourself, the Prime Native. Avatars of other people exist in your heart, mind, or both.

Your inner life survival kit contains all the trinkets you need to negotiate safe passage with these avatars. One of the most potent of these trinkets is your Talisman. To illustrate its importance, consider the example of the late Leonard Cohen, the Canadian singer-songwriter. Cohen was known to carry a small notebook wherever he went. This notebook served as his talisman, a physical object that connected him to his inner life. In it, he jotted down lyrics, observations, and reflections that later became some of his most famous songs. The notebook was more than just a collection of pages; it was a gateway to his inner world, a tool that helped him navigate the complexities of his thoughts and emotions.

Remember that your inner life is entirely yours. It is a dreamscape, a land of imagination, and a construct of your inner self. Everything and everyone you encounter in your inner life is a part of your own awareness. Each avatar of another person is simply a part of yourself that you have allowed to be a part of your inner life.

You can think of yourself as a 'holistic self' with many different avatars. These avatars can either be in balance with the rest of your inner life or out of balance. They can be symbiotic or destructive.

Hating any avatar in your inner life is self-destructive. Instead, in a peaceful state of mind, allow everything in your inner life to simply exist. Your Talisman, like Cohen's notebook, can serve as a physical reminder of this principle, helping you to maintain a balanced and harmonious inner life.

Equipped with the essential tools from the Interior Life Survival Kit, let's explore how these tools manifest in real-world leadership.

On Your Voyage of Discovery, Remember

Encounter everything with equanimous awareness and tentative acceptance. Remember that everything in your inner life, even the destructive parts, deserves to be treated with kindness. Use discernment to carefully separate the symbiotic from the parasitic and address each accordingly. Actively listen, with an open heart, to the answers you receive when you are speaking with the avatars within yourself. This is a practice of self-acceptance and self-awareness. You have everything each avatar within you needs, even if you do not realize it. Trust that everything happening within you is happening for you, not to you. Be kind to yourself and all of your avatars.

As we close this chapter, let us remember that leadership is not merely about what we do but who we are. Our actions may define us in the eyes of the world, but it's our interior life that shapes these actions and gives them meaning. The 'Interior Life Survival Kit' is not just a set of tools; it's a holistic approach to leadership that starts from within. By tending to our inner lives, we not only become better leaders but also better human beings. So, as you step forward in your leadership journey, keep in mind that the most important terrain you'll ever conquer is the landscape within.

KEY TAKEAWAYS

- The interior life of a leader is crucial for their ability to handle setbacks and maintain calm in crises. This involves a life of prayer and living in the presence of God.
- Leaders need to tend to their inner lives, ensuring it is free of psychological pitfalls and spiritual hazards. This involves allocating resources for retreats, engaging mentors and coaches, and cultivating a rich interior life.
- The Interior Life Survival Kit is a set of tools for leaders to navigate their interior life. This includes a sharp knife (Discernment), Guide, Granola, Game plan, Talisman, Journal, and Trinkets.
- Discernment is essential for leaders to separate what is essential to them and respond appropriately, ensuring they always have enough time for the things that matter most.
- Leaders need to keep a record of their inner journey, which can serve as a useful map of the topography of a human life.
- Leaders will encounter representations of other people in their inner life, and they need to negotiate safe passage with these avatars using trinkets.

ACTION ITEMS

- Cultivate a life of prayer and living in the presence of God. This will help you handle setbacks and maintain calm in crises.
- Allocate necessary resources to go on retreats, engage mentors and coaches, and cultivate a rich interior life.
- Use the tools in the Interior Life Survival Kit to navigate your interior life. This includes practicing discernment, engaging with a guide, eating healthily (Granola), creating a game plan, using a talisman, keeping a journal, and using trinkets.
- Practice discernment when presented with a new opportunity or task. This will ensure you always have enough time for the things that matter most.
- Keep a journal of your inner journey. This will help you recall where you started, how far you have come, and all that has happened along the way.
- Negotiate safe passage with the avatars in your inner life using trinkets. Remember to treat everything in your inner life with kindness.

CHAPTER 20

Conative Clarity

Enhancing Leadership Through Understanding

In this chapter, we will delve into the intricacies of human motivation and how understanding it can significantly enhance your leadership skills. We will explore the concept of "Method of Operation" (MO) as defined according to "Kolbe Wisdom," and how better aligning a person's MO with their roles can boost motivation and productivity. We will also touch upon the psychological theories that offer a deeper understanding of motivation. Let's begin by examining how a nuanced understanding of how one's MO can unlock their full potential.

The Science of Conative Awareness: Kolbe's Method of Operation ("MO")

Leadership is not merely about giving orders; it's about understanding what fuels your team's drive and aligning it with organizational goals. This alignment of individual tendencies with role-specific tasks is what Kolbe Corp refers to as the "Method of Operation" or "MO".

Kolbe Corp, a pioneering team of psychologists specializing in the conative aspect of the mind, has developed a framework to understand this better. The conative mind is the facet of mental life that is geared towards action, striving, and desire. By tapping into your team's natural strengths as identified by Kolbe, you can elevate levels of productivity, comfort, and overall success.

The MO is broken down into four key aspects:

1. **Fact Finder**: Pertains to how individuals gather and disseminate information.

2. **Follow Thru**: Focuses on organizational and design skills.

3. **Quick Start**: Relates to an individual's comfort level with risk and uncertainty.

4. **Implementor**: Concerns how one interacts with space and tangible objects.

When an individual's MO is in harmony with the MO required for their role or task, they are not just likely but almost certain to excel. As a leader, your role is to facilitate this alignment, thereby enhancing productivity, fostering collaboration, and improving communication within your team.

Practical Application: Implementing MO in Your Team

If you're wondering how to put this knowledge into practice, whether in a professional setting or even within your family, rest assured that Kolbe Corp provides a wealth of resources. These tools can help you align your team members' MOs with the roles, projects, and tasks at hand. By embracing this understanding, you unlock a reservoir of motivation and productivity that can propel your team to new heights.

For a deeper dive into how you can build a team that not only works well together but also thrives, visit Kolbe Corp's website. Remember, assembling the right team goes beyond merely hiring individuals who are intellectually gifted or personable. It's about unlocking the latent potential within each team member by becoming aware of how they naturally expend their mental energy.

> **"Learn your theories as well as you can, but put them aside when you touch the miracle of the living soul."**
> -- CARL JUNG

The Complexity of Human Motivation, Jungian Perspectives

The realm of human motivation is a labyrinthine subject that has fascinated psychologists for generations. While many have devoted their lifetimes to unraveling the enigmas behind human behavior, the field remains in awe of the intricate tapestry that constitutes motivation. To delve deeper into this subject, we turn to the work of

Carl Gustav Jung, a psychologist whose theories offer a rich framework for understanding motivation.

Jung diverges significantly from his contemporary, Sigmund Freud, who primarily emphasized the role of sexual drives in human behavior. Instead, Jung focused on the mysteries of the unconscious mind and the role of archetypes in shaping human actions and reactions. Indeed, modern attachment theory owes a greater debt to Jung than to Freud.

Jung introduced the concept of the "collective unconscious," a reservoir of emotionally charged experiences and wisdom inherited from our ancestors. This repository includes elements that may never have been part of our direct experience but have been transmitted through familial stories and cultural attitudes.

In Jung's framework, archetypes are universal, innate templates for behavior and personality that significantly influence human actions. These archetypes, according to Jung, are ancient reservoirs of human wisdom passed down through generations.

The Three Pillars of Motivation: Seeing, Sharing, Supporting

In my perspective, effective motivation hinges on three key principles: seeing, sharing, and supporting.

Seeing: This involves recognizing and understanding an individual's relationship to the archetypes present in their collective unconscious. The more adept you are at this, the more the individual will feel genuinely seen and understood.

Sharing: This entails identifying mutually beneficial goals that align with both the motivator's and the individual's future aspirations. Agreement on these intermediate goals creates a shared vision for the future.

Supporting: This involves taking concrete steps to help the individual achieve their goals, steps that resonate with the archetypes they most strongly identify with and that are aligned with their ultimate, teleological ends.

In sum, understanding the interplay between the collective unconscious and archetypes can offer invaluable insights for those seeking to comprehend the human psyche and effectively motivate others. By applying the principles of seeing, sharing, and supporting, you can tap into deeper layers of motivation, thereby enriching both individual and collective endeavors.

The Energies of 'How' and 'Why'

Understanding the dynamic interplay between an individual's natural tendencies for task accomplishment—known as their Method of Operation (MO)—and their ongoing journey toward self-realization is crucial. A holistic approach, one that considers the cognitive, affective, and conative aspects of the human mind, is indispensable for maximizing both individual and collective potential.

Effective motivators do more than merely incentivize; they tap into the very core of an individual's identity and aspirations. They inspire people to live authentically and take meaningful steps toward their goals. This art of motivation, particularly in a leadership context, employs the three pillars of motivation—seeing, sharing, and supporting—to align an individual's MO and self-realization with the broader objectives of the organization, corporation, or community.

A myopic approach to leadership, one that fixates solely on short-term rewards and punishments, is a recipe for failure. Such an approach neglects the deeper, more fundamental human needs for self-actualization and meaningful engagement. In contrast, leadership that adopts a holistic approach not only satisfies these deeper needs but also inspires a level of devotion that can transform mere work into a meaningful endeavor aligned with shared goals.

Investing time and effort in cultivating personal relationships is not just beneficial; it's essential. The goal is to nurture "true believers"—individuals who are not just committed but are also convinced that their collaboration with the leader contributes to their own betterment. For any leader serious about their role, the acquisition and retention of such devoted followers should be a primary focus.

Motivating others is not a task to be rushed. While shortcuts may offer immediate gains, they invariably undermine long-term efforts and can erode trust. The hard work of genuinely investing in others pays off in the form of a team that is not just motivated but also deeply committed to the collective vision.

KEY TAKEAWAYS

- Understanding the natural tendencies or "method of operation" (MO) of your team members can significantly increase productivity, comfort, and success. This involves understanding how they gather and share information, how they organize and design, how they handle risk and uncertainty, and how they handle space and tangible things.
- Aligning a person's MO with the ideal MO for a role or task can lead to exceptional performance. This involves placing team members in positions that capitalize on their strengths.
- Human motivation is a complex and multifaceted subject that involves conscious thoughts, images held in the personal unconscious mind, and archetypes in the collective unconscious. Motivation can also be inspired by goals and aspirations for a future desired by the individual.
- The keys to motivating an individual are seeing, sharing, and supporting. This involves understanding the individual's relationship to the archetypes in the collective unconscious, identifying shared intermediate goals, and taking action to help the individual achieve their goals.
- A holistic approach to motivation that embraces self-actualization can inspire devotion and create meaningful work towards shared goals. This involves aligning a person's MO and self-realization with the organizational, corporate, or community goal.

ACTION ITEMS

- Understand the natural tendencies or "method of operation" (MO) of your team members. This can be done through resources like Kolbe Corp.
- Align your team members' MOs with the ideal MO for their role or task. This involves placing team members in positions that capitalize on their strengths.
- Understand the role of the collective unconscious and archetypes in shaping human motivation. This can provide valuable insight for motivating others.
- Use the keys to motivating an individual - seeing, sharing, and supporting - in your leadership approach. This involves understanding the individual's relationship to the archetypes in the collective unconscious, identifying shared intermediate goals, and taking action to help the individual achieve their goals.
- Take a holistic approach to motivation that embraces self-actualization. This involves aligning a person's MO and self-realization with the organizational, corporate, or community goal.
- Invest time and effort in personal relationships to cultivate true believers in your team. This involves gaining followers and motivating others through investment and understanding.

CHAPTER 21

Simplicity in Leadership

The Key to Effective Decision-Making

In 2021, NASA deployed Ingenuity, a helicopter-like drone, from the Perseverance Mars rover. Although NASA initially downplayed expectations by claiming that the drone was only meant to demonstrate technology using off-the-shelf components, Ingenuity still managed to complete 30 successful flights in 18 months. This success has inspired NASA to include two helicopter drones in their upcoming Mars sample return mission, which will help retrieve sample containers and load them into the rocket that will send them into orbit around Mars.

The remarkable journey of NASA's Ingenuity helicopter on Mars serves as more than just a technological triumph; it's a parable of essentialism in practice. Each decision in this mission, from the selection of components to the flight paths, was guided by a clear focus on what was truly vital for success. This approach mirrors the journey of a leader who must discern and act upon what is most critical in their endeavors. Reflect upon your current projects: What are the 'Ingenuity' elements in them that, if focused upon, could lead to breakthroughs?

The process of achieving your goals, no matter how big or small, requires the same discipline as what it took to fly a drone on Mars. At each stage of progress, it's essential to identify what is most important and prioritize your efforts accordingly. Every phase of progress should end with a milestone, a significant event that marks the completion of an essential step in the process. Anticipating each milestone is crucial for anyone who wants to achieve success efficiently and effectively.

> **"You cannot overestimate the unimportance of practically everything."**
> **-- JOHN MAXWELL**

The ingenuity demonstrated by NASA's Mars mission is a vivid illustration of essentialism in action. It's a testament to focusing on what truly matters to achieve remarkable results. This same principle underpins Greg McKeown's philosophy in 'Essentialism: The Disciplined Pursuit of Less.' Let's explore how this principle, when applied to our personal and professional lives, can lead to extraordinary outcomes.

ESSENTIALISM

In 2014, Greg McKeown published a phenomenal book, called *Essentialism: The Disciplined Pursuit of Less*. McKeown breaks down the book into four parts:

1. **"Essence,"** in which he asks and answers: "What is the Core Mind-Set of an Essentialist?"

2. **"Explore,"** in which he asks and answers: "How Can We Discern the Trivial Many from the Vital Few?"

3. **"Eliminate**," in which he asks and answers: "How Can We Cut Out the Trivial Many?"

4. **"Execute,"** in which he asks and answers: "How Can We Make Doing the Vital Few Things Almost Effortless?"

Diving deeper into McKeown's Essentialism, consider the case of a busy executive overwhelmed by tasks. By adopting the "Essence" mindset, he begins to question which of these tasks align with his core objectives. Through "Exploration," he discerns the vital few responsibilities. "Elimination" allows him to shed the non-essential, and "Execution" focuses his efforts on these chosen priorities, leading to enhanced productivity and satisfaction.

To do the vital work of identifying the essential, one would do very well to follow McKeown's formula. In Essentialism, McKeown starts by adopting a mindset that is well-suited to making good decisions, that is, rational choices based on one's personal values.

The Pareto Principle and the MED, though related, serve different purposes. Imagine a small business owner: applying the 80/20 rule, he finds that 80% of his profits come from 20% of his customers. Focusing on these customers is his 'vital few.' On the other hand, the MED approach could be used in his marketing efforts—determining the least amount of investment that yields maximum returns. Understanding where each principle applies best can transform his business strategy.

Embracing McKeown's essentialism naturally leads us to another powerful concept: the Pareto Principle. This principle, like essentialism, is about distilling the abundance of choices to the most impactful few. Understanding the relationship between these concepts deepens our grasp of efficient and effective decision-making. McKeown mentions the "Pareto Principle"--sometimes also called "the 80/20 Rule"--introduced by Vilfredo Pareto as early as the 1790s, which states that for many outcomes, roughly 80% of consequences come from 20% of causes—the "vital few".[25]

McKeown introduces the principle of "less but better," which he distilled from Ferran Adrià, who he considers to be the world's greatest chef. The idea of "less but better" may prove challenging, especially for those who have been rewarded for doing more in the past. However, research shows that more effort does not always lead to better results. Instead, McKeown suggests focusing on the "vital few" things that consistently produce the best results, as opposed to the "trivial many" things that produce mediocre results.[26]

McKeown mentions the "Pareto Principle" (sometimes also called "the 80/20 Rule"), introduced by Vilfredo Pareto as early as the 1790s, which states that for many outcomes, roughly 80% of consequences come from 20% of causes—the "vital few".[27]

I first encountered the Pareto Principle in *The 4-Hour Workweek*, by Tim Ferriss, who also champions the "minimum effective dose" ("MED").

I want to point out, however, that the MED is more of a minimalist than an essentialist principle. The minimum effective does is the smallest amount of input required to produce—or, as some might prefer, "reliably produce"—a result. The MED and the "vital few" are not necessarily the same. I recommend focusing on the vital few for consistently better results.

"The overwhelming reality is: we live in a world where almost everything is worthless and a very few things are exceptionally valuable. As John Maxwell has written, 'You cannot overestimate the unimportance of practically everything.'"[28]

When Maxwell states, "You cannot overestimate the unimportance of practically everything," he's echoing a truth that resonates across fields. This sentiment is shared by many thought leaders, such as Marie Kondo in the realm of personal organization, who advocates for keeping only what "sparks joy," effectively applying essentialism to decluttering one's life. Such diverse perspectives enrich our understanding of focusing on what truly matters.

As McKeown puts it: "A non-essentialist thinks almost everything is essential," whereas, "An essentialist thinks almost everything is nonessential." I encourage you to become an essentialist.

The Pareto Principle's focus on the 'vital few' aligns closely with the essence of strategic trade-offs, a cornerstone of essentialism. Recognizing that we cannot excel at everything, and that every choice involves a trade-off, is vital for effective leadership and personal growth. Let's delve into how this understanding shapes our approach to challenges and opportunities.

Essentialism and Trade-Offs

The brilliant economist Thomas Sowell once famously wrote: "There are no solutions... only trade-offs."[29] Good leadership often involves choosing one set of circumstances over another for the benefit of a person or group. Essentialism involves embracing the truth that you cannot have it all and making a choice regarding the trade-offs. McKeown asks the question, "Which problem do I want?" This question embraces the truth: *One cannot have it all.*

Consider a community leader faced with limited resources and numerous demands. By applying essentialist principles, he must decide which community projects will yield the most benefit. This decision-making process involves weighing trade-offs: perhaps prioritizing a health initiative over a recreational project. Each choice reflects a commitment to the 'vital few' that promise the most significant impact for her community.

Identifying the essential to your goals means discovering the vital few causes that will consistently, efficiently, and effectively produce the results you desire and being willing to trade everything else for those things. The essentialist is comfortable with trading away 80% of potential causes, knowing that those will only produce the desired outcome 20% of the time.

In my work, I used to present the need to make a crucial decision regarding certain trade-offs by presenting the so-called "Iron Triangle" of "Cheap and Fast; Good and Cheap, or Good and Fast." I no longer do this.

Benek Lisefski's article, "The Big Lie of 'Good, Fast, Cheap,'" highlights the importance of striving for "Good + Fast."[30] Lisefski argues that "Cheap + Fast" is a waste of time and money, and that "Good + Cheap" doesn't exist. He emphasizes that "slower doesn't mean cheaper" and that "Fast + Good" is the only thing worth striving for.

In line with Lisefski's thoughts, the author recommends working in the realm of "Good, Fast, and Expensive." This requires being trusted as an expert in one's field and consistently delivering creative work that lives up to that expectation. The author suggests picking services from the top half of price quotes, as those are the ones who will deliver quality work.

What milestones do you foresee in your journey towards great leadership? Make a list, prioritize, review often, and adjust as needed. Keep in mind the principles of essentialism and Lisefski's thoughts on striving for "Good + Fast." These principles will help guide you towards making strategic decisions and reaching your goals efficiently and effectively.

As we reflect on these principles of essentialism, the Pareto Principle, and the importance of trade-offs, we come to see a clear path forward. These concepts not only illuminate the journey towards effective leadership but also offer practical steps we can take. Let us now distill these insights into key takeaways and actionable steps to apply in our quest for excellence.

KEY TAKEAWAYS

- Discipline in Goal Achievement: Just like the disciplined approach required to fly NASA's Ingenuity on Mars, achieving any goal demands identifying and prioritizing what is most important at each stage.
- Essentialism in Practice: Embrace the mindset of 'less but better', focusing on the 'vital few' tasks that yield the most significant results, as championed by Greg McKeown in "Essentialism: The Disciplined Pursuit of Less."
- Pareto Principle Application: Understand the Pareto Principle, or the 80/20 rule, which states that roughly 80% of consequences come from 20% of causes—focusing on these 'vital few' is key to effective leadership and decision-making.
- Importance of Trade-Offs: Recognize that leadership often involves strategic trade-offs; not everything can be achieved simultaneously, so prioritizing the most impactful tasks or decisions is essential.
- Quality and Speed Over Cost: Align with the principle of striving for 'Good + Fast' over 'Cheap + Fast' or 'Good + Cheap' to ensure quality outcomes in your endeavors.
- Reflective Analogy: Remember, like Ingenuity's focused design for its Mars mission, prioritizing the essential in your endeavors leads to breakthrough achievements.

ACTION ITEMS

- Prioritize Essential Tasks: Regularly identify and prioritize the most important tasks in your progress towards goals, ensuring each phase ends with a significant milestone.
- Weekly Essentialism Exercise: Conduct a weekly review of tasks, categorizing them under 'essential' and 'non-essential', and focus your upcoming week on the essential tasks.
- Apply the 80/20 Rule: Use the Pareto Principle in your decision-making process, focusing your efforts on the 20% of tasks or decisions that will produce 80% of your desired outcomes.
- Reflect on Decision-Making: Reflect on a recent decision involving prioritization. Assess how applying essentialism could have altered the process or outcome.
- Choose Quality and Speed: In your professional endeavors, aim for solutions that are 'Good + Fast', recognizing that this often leads to the most effective and high-quality results.
- Adjust Milestones Regularly: Continuously review and adjust your list of milestones, keeping the principles of essentialism and the focus on 'Good + Fast' at the forefront.

CHAPTER 22

Transformative Receptivity

Mastering Leadership through Feedback

As a leader, your ability to influence others is closely tied to your level of receptivity, which I refer to as "influenceability." The best leaders are highly receptive to feedback, new ideas, and diverse opinions, even if they challenge the status quo. Your ability to influence others, therefore, is tied to your own influenceability.

Consider the story of David, a CEO of a successful startup. Known for his no-nonsense approach, David was often perceived as unapproachable, rarely accepting feedback from his team. This changed when his wife pointed out the limitations of his leadership style. Taking this feedback to heart, David began to listen more actively to his employees, granting them greater autonomy. This shift not only improved team collaboration and innovation but also led to increased employee satisfaction and enhanced business outcomes, illustrating the profound impact receptivity to feedback can have on a leader's influence.

David's transformation underscores a broader truth in leadership: the power of receptivity extends far beyond individual cases. It's a fundamental attribute of influential leaders everywhere.

> **"Avoiding feedback is a path to stagnation, not growth."**

The Significance of Your Attitude towards Feedback

When you think about receiving feedback, how do you feel? What associations come to mind? Take a moment to jot down your thoughts. While leaders' receptivity is crucial, equally important is their approach to handling feedback. This not only involves internalizing feedback but also actively engaging with it.

Many leaders react negatively to feedback, often feeling defensive due to a perception that their abilities are under attack. However, it's crucial to restructure this perception and view feedback as a growth opportunity. Recognizing feedback as constructive rather than personal criticism can transform it from a source of discomfort into a valuable tool for development.

However, avoiding feedback is a path to stagnation, not growth. As a leader, it's important to restructure your negative associations with feedback and view it as valuable and constructive insight. If you see feedback as a personal attack, your amygdala will activate, leading to a defensive response and resistance to accepting feedback.

Leaders often face hurdles in becoming receptive, such as inherent biases and preconceived notions. To overcome these, it's crucial to actively challenge one's own perspectives and remain open to alternative viewpoints. Encouraging an environment where feedback is not just accepted but solicited can transform these challenges into opportunities for growth and learning.

In fact, many businesses and high-performing individuals pay for feedback, recognizing that it reveals what is working well and what needs improvement, essential information for those committed to continual growth. Understanding the theory behind feedback is just the beginning. The true test for leaders lies in its practical application, as exemplified by some of the world's most successful leaders.

Embracing feedback has been a key driver of success for several renowned leaders. Satya Nadella, CEO of Microsoft, transformed the company's culture by fostering openness to feedback, thus revitalizing Microsoft's innovation and employee engagement. Jeff Bezos of Amazon attributes much of his company's success to its customer feedback-oriented approach, demonstrating how external feedback can guide strategic decisions. Bill Gates, co-founder of Microsoft, consistently sought feedback from his employees, a practice that has been fundamental to his ability to adapt and lead effectively.

Leaders with strong character demonstrate a high receptivity to feedback, particularly when constructive. They understand the value of all feedback, good and bad, as part of a continuous growth and accountability system, and learn from the substance of the feedback beyond its tone.

Great leaders possess a high level of receptivity, being open to feedback, new ideas, and diverse opinions. This openness can present unique challenges, especially if these ideas are accepted by a minority or a group with limited decision-making power. But for the purposes of this chapter, we will refer to all three as simply "feedback."

Embracing Feedback

Proclaiming an open door policy for feedback is only meaningful if leaders genuinely embrace it. Punishing or ignoring those who provide challenging feedback indicates poor leadership and erodes trust. True leaders value all feedback, showing gratitude and respect for the courage it takes to deliver, which in turn deepens trust and fosters open communication.

Leaders with an open door policy for feedback show their followers that they value their ideas, opinions, and voices, and that they are willing to make changes based on their considerations. As a leader, it's desirable to receive feedback from everyone, even if it may not be immediately recognized as constructive. With strength, you can sift through the unhelpful parts and find valuable insights.

If receiving feedback is difficult for you, understand that it's normal. As a leader, however, it's important to master difficult conversations. People take a risk when they bring you feedback, and it's important to appreciate and acknowledge their courage. Facilitate the conversation, address conflicts that arise, and work through what could be a difficult situation in a collaborative way. This will result in more diverse perspectives and a deeper understanding of what is needed for growth.

Most importantly, embracing feedback will deepen trust between you and your followers, demonstrating that you care about their opinions and perspectives, and that you are taking them into consideration. When others feel heard, they will have more confidence in your ability to make informed decisions and will be more likely to follow your lead. Learning to navigate difficult conversations and cultivating influenceability also makes it easier to lead your team in a collaborative and responsive way. Your influence depends on your influenceability, and the best leaders are extremely receptive to feedback, new ideas, and divergent opinions. Leaders with strong character and a commitment to continual improvement are highly receptive to feedback, especially when it is constructive. They welcome all feedback, and understand that it is an integral part of a system of accountability and continual growth that serves leaders and those who follow them.

It is important for leaders to recognize that feedback is not always positive, but it reveals what is working well and what is not. This information is necessary for those committed to continual improvement. Leaders who are resilient and committed to improvement welcome all feedback, and are hungry for it. They sift through the good and the bad, the triggering and the nurturing, and they learn from the substance of what has been communicated.

Great leaders seek not only constructive feedback, but receive all feedback with grace and in a spirit of gratitude. Receiving feedback demonstrates to followers that their leader values their ideas, opinions, and voices, and is willing to make changes as a result of their considerations. Leaders who listen to and acknowledge feedback and give followers reasons to believe they have a voice will deepen trust between themselves and those who follow them.

It is also important for leaders to understand that people take a risk when they bring them feedback they suspect they do not want to hear. Leaders should appreciate and acknowledge their courage and make a decent effort to facilitate the conversation and address any conflicts that may arise. This will result in more diverse perspectives, a deeper understanding of what needs to happen to grow towards goals, and an enhancement to efficiency and effectiveness.

Receptivity to feedback also demands mastery in navigating complex interpersonal dynamics, particularly when conversations are challenging.

Mastering difficult conversations is a vital skill for leaders. This involves not just active listening but also creating a safe space where team members feel comfortable voicing their concerns. Leaders should approach these conversations with empathy, seeking to understand rather than to respond defensively. Acknowledging the courage it takes to provide feedback and addressing any resulting conflicts constructively can foster a culture of open communication and mutual respect.

Your influenceability, or receptivity, is a valuable and powerful trait for a leader. It demonstrates to your followers that you care about their voices and perspectives, and it makes it easier to lead your team in a collaborative and responsive way. Your influence depends on your influenceability, so strive to welcome all feedback, navigate difficult conversations, and cultivate a spirit of receptivity and continual improvement.

KEY TAKEAWAYS

- Influence Through Receptivity: A leader's influence is directly linked to their receptivity or "influenceability," which involves openness to diverse feedback, ideas, and opinions, fostering innovation and growth.
- Transformational Impact of Receptivity: Embracing feedback, as demonstrated by leaders like Satya Nadella and Bill Gates, can transform a leader's effectiveness and lead to significant organizational improvements.
- Constructive Approach to Feedback: Restructuring negative perceptions of feedback and viewing it as an opportunity for growth is crucial for avoiding stagnation and fostering a positive leadership environment.
- Value of Open Communication: Maintaining an authentic open-door policy for feedback, without punishing or ignoring dissenting voices, builds trust and encourages honest communication within the team.
- Mastering Difficult Conversations: Skillfully navigating challenging conversations and creating a supportive environment for feedback is key to deepening trust and understanding within a team.
- Feedback as a Continuous Growth Tool: Regularly seeking and valuing feedback, both positive and constructive, is integral for continual self-improvement and effective leadership.

ACTION ITEMS

- Cultivate Influenceability: Actively cultivate a high level of influenceability by being open and responsive to feedback, new ideas, and diverse opinions, recognizing their value in driving change and innovation.
- Implement Feedback Exercises: Regularly schedule exercises to seek and process feedback, using it to make informed decisions and improvements, similar to the practices of successful leaders.
- Develop Feedback Handling Skills: Work on developing skills for handling challenging feedback, including active listening, empathetic responses, and constructive conflict resolution.
- Engage in Reflective Practices: Engage in regular self-reflection to assess and improve your receptivity to feedback, considering how your responses and actions influence your leadership effectiveness.
- Facilitate Open Communication: Ensure that your open-door policy is genuine and inclusive, encouraging team members to share feedback without fear of negative consequences.
- Acknowledge and Appreciate Courage: Show appreciation and acknowledge the courage of team members who provide feedback, especially when it challenges your views or approaches.

CHAPTER 23

The Smart Fail Approach

Transforming Leadership through Setbacks

In your experience of leadership, every setback or loss is not a dead-end but a valuable source of feedback. This perspective transforms failures from discouraging end-points to crucial stepping stones in our path to success.

As a leader, it's natural to strive for success in everything you do. But what happens when you experience a setback or loss, either personal or professional? It can be difficult to bounce back and regain your confidence as a leader. However, it's important to remember that failure is not the end; it's simply a part of the journey towards success. In this chapter, we'll explore ways to redeem failures and turn them into valuable feedback to help you become a better leader.

Embracing Failure for Growth

Failures, when approached with the right mindset, become less about blame and more about valuable lessons learned. It's not just about what went wrong, but what can be done better next time.

The way you view failures can have a big impact on how you respond to them. It's important to understand that not all failures are created equal. Some failures can actually be praiseworthy if they result in useful feedback. By shifting your mindset and viewing failures as opportunities to learn, you can become more resilient in the face of adversity.

> **"Instead of making excuses for failure, focus on what you learned from the experience."**

Failing Smarter

To have more praiseworthy failures, it's important to learn how to have productive discussions about failures. This means breaking away from the negative associations of "failure" and "success" and instead focusing on the results of your efforts. When you focus on the outcome, you'll be less likely to engage in blaming others, ignoring your own contributions, criticizing others, or denying that success was ever an option.

Instead of making excuses for failure, focus on what you learned from the experience. What was the result of your attempt? What did you learn about yourself and your own contributions? By doing some detective work and understanding the cause-and-effect dynamics at play, you'll be better equipped to handle future failures in a more intelligent way.

To have more praiseworthy failures, it's important to create processes that make room for smart failure. This means incorporating failure into your planning process and having a predetermined response to foreseeable causes of failure. When you plan for failure, you'll be better prepared to pivot when failures inevitably occur.

Failing Smarter-er

Being a leader means taking 100% responsibility for everything in your experience. Even if some things are not 100% your fault, pretending that they are can help you become more empowered and lead with confidence in any situation. This doesn't mean that you shouldn't collaborate with others, but instead, it means accepting responsibility for your circumstances and inviting your team to do the same.

It's important to communicate your strategy for adapting to foreseeable failures and to make sure everyone on your team is on the same page about shared goals, how failures will be communicated, maintaining professional detachment, examining different angles of a situation, and making meaningful changes based on what your team learns from the failure. By creating a "fail-safe" environment, you'll boost emotional safety and create a culture of transparency and accountability.

Failing Smart-li-est

In order to truly embrace failure as a valuable learning experience, it's important to adopt the mindset of a research scientist rather than a manager. This means embracing the Smart Fail Cycle, a scientific process that begins with failure and leads to continuous improvement.

THE SMART FAIL CYCLE:

- Fail: Own the failure, take 100% responsibility for it, and be intentional about learning everything you can from the experience.

- Learn: Get curious and take detailed notes, assess your understanding, feedback systems, and adaptation processes.

- Improve: Based on what you learned, project onto your current operations how things could be better and champion those improvements.

- Try Again: Apply what you learned, make a meaningful change, and attempt to achieve the desired result in a different and more intelligent way.

Having established the mindset shift necessary for viewing failure as feedback, let's explore how this approach is put into practice in leading organizations.

Embracing Failure with Strategic Insights

The 'Smart Fail Cycle' is more than a concept; it's a practice adopted by industry leaders. For instance, IBM's 'Continuous Relevance Program' initiated in 2014, marks a strategic shift, encouraging employees to innovate, take risks, and importantly, learn from failures. This program equips staff with tools to analyze and grow from setbacks, fostering a culture where experimentation is valued over playing it safe.

Similarly, at Amazon, CEO Jeff Bezos champions a culture where failure is not just accepted but seen as essential to innovation. Amazon's approach involves starting with customer needs and working backward, a methodology that welcomes risks and learns from missteps in product and service development. This ethos has propelled Amazon to the forefront of e-commerce and technology, making it a prime example of success born from a willingness to fail.

Google, too, implements the Smart Fail Cycle in its operations. Known for its encouraging attitude towards risk-taking and experimentation, Google employs a systematic 'post-mortem' process. This approach involves detailed analysis of failures to pinpoint areas for improvement, fostering an environment where each setback is viewed as an opportunity for growth and innovation.

These cases from IBM, Amazon, and Google demonstrate that the Smart Fail Cycle is a vital component of modern business strategy, turning failures into stepping stones for success. Now that we've seen how industry leaders apply the Smart Fail Cycle, let's turn our attention to how we can foster this culture within our own teams.

Adopting the Smart Fail Cycle

By embracing the Smart Fail Cycle, you'll become more innovative and equipped to lead with resilience and success.

As a leader, it's important to recognize that failure is a natural part of the growth process, and it's not something to be ashamed of. The key to success lies in how you respond to failure and use it to your advantage. By changing your mindset from viewing failure as a negative outcome to viewing it as valuable feedback, you'll be able to learn from your experiences and make smarter decisions moving forward.

One of the biggest mistakes leaders make is to focus on blaming others, ignoring their own contributions to the failure, criticizing others' shortcomings, and denying that success was ever a viable option. This type of mindset not only hinders your ability to grow and improve, but it also undermines the confidence and trust of your team. Instead, it's crucial to focus on results and what you learned from the experience.

To have more praiseworthy failures, you need to get good at failing. This means conducting a thorough investigation of what went wrong, identifying the cause-and-effect dynamics at play, and figuring out what you can do differently next time. The Smart Fail Cycle provides a structured approach for doing just that.

Step one of the Smart Fail Cycle is to "Fail." This is where you take ownership of the failure, accept 100% responsibility, and focus on learning everything you can from the experience. Step two is "Learn." Get curious, take detailed notes, and continuously assess your operational understanding, feedback systems, and adaptation processes. Step three is "Improve." Use what you learned to make improvements to your current operations, and be excited about the progress you're making.

Step four of the Smart Fail Cycle is "Try Again." This is where you apply what you learned, make a meaningful change, and attempt to achieve the result you're seeking. It's important to note that this stage is not just about trying harder, it's about trying in a more intelligent way. By continuously refining your approach, you'll increase your chances of success.

Fostering a Team Culture for "Smart Failure"

To fully embrace the Smart Fail Cycle, it's essential to not only understand it conceptually but to apply it consistently across all aspects of leadership and team dynamics. Successful failure management is not just an individual effort but a team endeavor. By creating an environment where team members feel safe to share and learn from failures, we build a resilient and innovative team culture.

To this end, it's important to clearly communicate your failure strategy, including its related goals and values, to your team and create a culture of openness and transparency. It's crucial for leaders to transparently communicate their strategies for dealing with failures. This involves setting clear expectations, creating an open feedback loop, and ensuring that every team member understands and participates in the process of learning from failures.

Encourage your team to embrace the Smart Fail Cycle and take calculated risks together. Make sure everyone is on the same page about shared goals, how failures will be communicated, maintaining professional detachment, and continually improving based on what you learned from failures.

It's also helpful to regularly assess your failure strategy to see if it's working or if it needs to be adjusted. Don't be afraid to ask others how they handle failures, and seek feedback from those who are better at failing than you are. There's always room for improvement, and by continually learning and growing, you'll become a more effective leader.

In this chapter, we've explored how viewing failure as feedback can transform our leadership approach. From the mindset shift to embracing the Smart Fail Cycle, and from individual application to fostering a supportive team environment, we've covered how to turn setbacks into growth opportunities.

Don't be afraid of failure. Embrace it as an opportunity to learn, grow, and become a better leader. By using the Smart Fail Cycle, you'll be able to turn failures into praiseworthy experiences that will help you achieve greater success in the future.

KEY TAKEAWAYS

- Redefining Failure: Recognize that failure is a critical component of the leadership journey, offering opportunities for learning and growth, not just setbacks.
- Outcome-Oriented Approach: Emphasize the importance of focusing on outcomes and lessons learned from failures, moving beyond blame and excuses.
- Responsibility and Empowerment: Highlight the empowerment that comes from taking 100% responsibility for all experiences, even when not entirely at fault.
- Smart Fail Cycle: Outline the Smart Fail Cycle (failing, learning, improving, trying again) as a methodical process for turning failures into continuous improvement opportunities.
- Role of Communication: Stress the need for clear communication and transparency in dealing with failures, ensuring team alignment on goals, failure communication, and learning processes.
- Learning from Industry Leaders: Draw attention to how industry giants like IBM, Amazon, and Google utilize the Smart Fail Cycle, demonstrating its practical application in diverse business environments.

ACTION ITEMS

- Adopt a Growth Mindset: Actively shift your perspective to view failures as valuable learning opportunities, essential for growth and innovation.

  - Recognize Fixed Mindset Triggers: Pay attention to moments when you feel threatened or defensive about failures. These are indicators of a fixed mindset.

  - Reframe Challenges as Opportunities: Whenever you encounter a failure, consciously reframe it in your mind as an opportunity to learn something new or improve a skill.

  - Seek Constructive Feedback: Regularly ask for feedback, not just during successes but more importantly during failures. Use this feedback to identify areas for growth.

  - Celebrate Learning, Not Just Success: Make a habit of acknowledging and celebrating the learning process itself, not just the successful outcomes.

  - Set Learning Goals: Instead of only setting performance-based goals, establish specific learning goals related to areas where you or your team can improve.

  - Reflect on Failures Constructively: After a setback, take time to reflect on what happened. Ask yourself: What did this experience teach me? How can I apply these lessons in the future?

- Analyze Outcomes and Lessons: In every failure, focus on understanding the outcomes and extracting key lessons, rather than resorting to blame.
- Assume Full Responsibility: Cultivate a mindset of full responsibility for all your experiences, fostering a sense of empowerment and proactive leadership.
- Implement the Smart Fail Cycle: Incorporate the Smart Fail Cycle into your leadership approach, using it as a framework for learning and improvement from failures.
- Communicate Failure Strategies: Effectively communicate your strategies for handling foreseeable failures to your team, establishing a shared understanding and approach.
- Continuous Strategy Assessment: Regularly evaluate the effectiveness of your failure strategy, seeking feedback and learning from others to enhance your approach to leadership challenges.

CHAPTER 24

Beneath the Surface

Tapping into Unseen Leadership Resources

In the previous chapters, we've delved into understanding our purpose, identifying our leadership traits, uncovering blind spots, and embracing disruption. Reflecting on these lessons has begun to deepen your awareness of your leadership capacity. Now, it's time to take stock of the resources you may not even be aware of—resources often buried beneath insecurities, false narratives, and limiting beliefs. This chapter is dedicated to guiding you in uncovering these hidden assets, enabling you to harness them effectively on your leadership journey. As we progress, you'll build a solid foundation for becoming a stronger, more impactful leader, ready to leverage your unique abilities through the exercises and reflections that follow.

Now, let's take a step further and ask ourselves, "What do I do best?" Answering this question will help you surface a surprising amount of value and skills you have to offer as a leader. To help you with this exercise, you can complete a few sentences that will guide you in articulating your strengths and experiences.

As you explore the following prompts, remember that each response builds a clearer picture of your unique leadership style.

- As a leader, the most helpful thing I do for others is: __________

- The example I am most proud of is when I: __________

- Most people wouldn't think a [your job title] would do things like __________, but I couldn't do things like [your first answer] without that skill.

- I feel a great deal of compassion for __________, which is why I am passionate about serving them as a [your job title].

- If you have ever encountered a situation in which you've needed someone to [your first answer], you know that someone who does that __________ is pretty rare.

- The best compliment I ever received was: __________

By answering these questions, you will gain a clearer understanding of your strengths and how to communicate them to others in a compelling and relatable way. Avoid using technical jargon and use active, not passive voice to describe what you do. Embrace your passion and let it shine through your words.

With this enhanced self-awareness, now, let's delve deeper into self-reflection, a tool indispensable in revealing your leadership strengths.

THE GIBBS REFLECTIVE CYCLE

Self-reflection can be a challenging process, but it is essential to uncovering the hidden treasures within yourself. To assist you in this journey, consider using the Gibbs Reflective Cycle, a model developed by American psychologist Graham Gibbs in his book "Learning by Doing."

The Reflective Cycle encourages you to think about, feel into, and base present actions on specific past experiences. It has six phases

1. Describe an experience that shaped you as a leader (or person);

2. Explore the feelings present during the experience;

3. Label the experience as "good" or "bad";

4. Consider the practical lessons the experience taught you and how it informed your decisions going forward;

5. Examine your actions from a perspective of emotional distance, acknowledging both positive and negative outcomes and alternative outcomes that could have resulted from different choices; and

6. Make a well-considered resolution to behave the same or differently in the future, based on the results of your reflection.

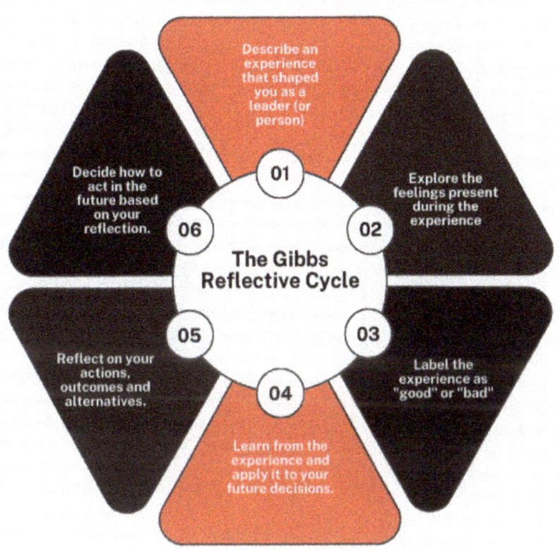

For instance, when reflecting on a challenging project, a leader might recognize feelings of frustration (Explore feelings), label it as a learning experience (Label the experience), and realize that proactive communication could have changed the outcome (Examine actions). Such reflections lead to a resolve for improved communication strategies in future projects (Resolution).

By using the Gibbs Reflective Cycle, you will gain a deeper appreciation of your personal experiences and the valuable lessons they have taught you. This process can be done independently, but many people benefit from the help of a mentor, coach, or guide. Don't hesitate to seek support if you need it.

Understanding your strengths is not just about self-awareness; it's deeply connected to emotional intelligence. It enables you to navigate the complex dynamics of leadership with resilience and adaptability.

> **"Asking for help is not a sign of weakness, but rather a hallmark of a great leader."**

A Solid Foundation

By completing the exercises in this chapter and using the Gibbs Reflective Cycle, you will have a clear, well-articulated understanding of your strengths and experiences, and a deeper appreciation of the valuable resources within you. This will provide a solid foundation for your journey towards becoming a stronger and more effective leader.

Remember, asking for help is not a sign of weakness, but rather a hallmark of a great leader. In fact, seeking outside perspectives from a mentor or coach can provide valuable accountability, transparency, and inter-subjective viewpoints that can greatly enhance your growth and development as a leader.

By now, you have likely gained a clearer understanding of your unique leadership strengths and the experiences that have shaped you as a leader. You have also learned the importance of reflective thinking and the power of self-awareness in surfacing your hidden resources. These insights and tools will serve as a firm foundation for the rest of your journey towards restoring or improving your leadership capacity.

Take these insights and tools and apply them. Reflect, grow, and step into your next chapter of leadership with confidence and a renewed sense of purpose.

In the coming chapters, we will delve deeper into the journey of leadership, exploring the many facets of effective leadership and the skills required to lead with excellence. We will also examine the importance of resilience and emotional intelligence in navigating the challenges of leadership. Most importantly, we will focus on the process of growth and development, and the steps you can take to continually improve as a leader.

Before moving on, however, take a deep breath, relax, and be proud of the progress you have made so far. You have taken the first step towards a new chapter in your leadership journey, and the future is bright. With the right mindset, the right tools, and the right support, you will soon find yourself leading with confidence, clarity, and purpose.

KEY TAKEAWAYS

- Uncover Hidden Strengths: Recognize the untapped resources within you to enhance your leadership effectiveness.
- Embrace Self-Reflection: Utilize structured reflection to gain insights into your leadership style and decision-making processes.
- Apply the Gibbs Reflective Cycle: Use this six-phase model to analyze your experiences and extract valuable lessons for personal growth.
- Value External Support: Seek guidance from mentors or coaches to gain diverse perspectives and accelerate your development.
- Articulate Your Leadership Capabilities: Clearly defining your strengths and experiences helps communicate your leadership value proposition effectively.
- Leverage Self-Awareness: Use your deepened self-awareness to navigate leadership challenges with resilience and adaptability.

ACTION ITEMS

- Identify Leadership Strengths: Reflect on what you do best as a leader and document the skills and value you offer.
- Engage with the Gibbs Reflective Cycle: Systematically work through each phase to derive meaning from past experiences and inform future actions.
- Pursue Mentorship: Actively seek out mentors or coaches to provide accountability and offer new viewpoints on your leadership approach.
- Maintain a Reflective Practice: Dedicate regular time for reflection, using structured methods to continuously evolve as a leader.
- Communicate Your Progress: Share your journey of self-discovery and learning with your team, encouraging a culture of growth and transparency.
- Celebrate Your Leadership Journey: Acknowledge and take healthy pride in your growth, staying motivated for ongoing improvement and success.

CHAPTER 25

Fit to Lead

Wellness in Leadership

What is presented in this chapter is going to be poorly accepted by some people, because the focus of this chapter addresses the way things are, right now, not the way some people think things ought to be.

Researchers studying discrimination against people on the basis of their weight have "found that implicit and explicit attitudes on the basis of sexuality, race, skin tone, age, and disability all remained the same or improved (showing a decrease in bias), while implicit bias on the basis of body weight increased 15 percent in less than a decade. Bias against fat people isn't on the way out—it's on the rise."[31]

Statistics show that overweight or obese people are more likely to be fired, passed up for a job, and paid less.[32] In the U.S., out of 50 states, only Michigan legally prohibits weight discrimination.

While recent legislation in New York and Massachusetts may expand legal protection to tens of millions of Americans, in most of the country, one can still (legally) be fired for being overweight or obese.[33] Overweight and obese people "face bias in every corner of life. They're more likely to be bullied in school, stigmatized by doctors, and convicted of crimes by juries. Survey respondents rate people who look overweight as lazier, weaker-willed, and less likely to win on *Jeopardy!*"[34]

"When the humiliations extend to the workplace, the costs can be all the more easily measured in dollars and cents. People who are overweight are hired less, promoted less, and paid less. One study suggests that for every 6 pounds an average American woman gains, her hourly pay drops 2%. And people signing paychecks subject heavier workers to a gauntlet of additional punishment, coercion, and harassment. 'It is endemic,' says Claudia Center, the legal director for the Disability Rights Education & Defense Fund, an advocacy group in Berkeley, Calif. One of her past clients, a cable installer, got risky weight-loss surgery after his company banned him from returning to work unless he lost about 100 pounds.

A Note of Compassion

To all those who are in the "fat acceptance movement," the author wants to say: I see you, I understand your struggle, I have compassion for you, and I am not here to shame you. That being said, getting people to ignore their perceptions and the heuristics that govern much of their thinking is essentially fighting human nature. While I genuinely wish you good luck in your efforts, I have very little optimism for the fat acceptance movement's long-term success.

His bosses thought he was too heavy to use their ladder, and they wanted to keep the ladder."[35]

In my opinion, rational compassion[36] ought to compel one to acknowledge that physically unfit people have unique challenges and that kindness and loving concern for the health and welfare of others is the best foundation on which to rest our thinking, speech, and actions towards them.

Nevertheless, the incontrovertible fact remains that people tend to associate good leadership with physical fitness.

> **"Bias against fat people isn't on the way out—it's on the rise."**

Professional Gains

Investing time and effort into eating healthy food and portions and in healthy physical exercise will improve your professional life. Not only will you have more energy and focus, you'll be more passionate and creative when tackling your work-related challenges each day.

Leaders need every advantage they can get. An observable trait of good leaders, therefore, tends to be a basic, if not intense, commitment to physical fitness.

If you're worried that you'll have to redirect too much time and energy to working out, which will cost you productivity at work, consider that each hour of work will be more productive when you have higher energy and a clearer mind, not to mention having to take fewer days off to recover from illness, because your body's immune system functions better when you're healthy.

Move to More Meaningful Meetings

Think about the last time you were in a meeting with someone who was lethargic, inattentive, and uninspired. How did that feel?

Now, think about the last time you were that person. How does that feel? Not great, right?

When you regularly and consistently move your body, your brain health improves. Not only does your body feel better, your mental energy levels increase, your focus gets sharper, and inspiration comes more naturally.

These effects make far easier your efforts to connect with others, share enjoyable interactions, and maintain a positive mood. Better physical health leads to better connections with others, because of the internal change in you, not just because people will see you differently (although they will).

The Athletic Mind

Leaders play an important role in ensuring processes run smoothly and their teams accomplish their goals. To be effective, leaders tend to have to simultaneously track many variables, endure high stress, and quickly recover from setbacks. The value of a sharp mind, therefore, cannot be overstated.

Research indicates improvements in cognitive function in people as young as 20 have been shown to have resulted from improvements in physical fitness.[37] Such improvements in cognitive function include, but are not limited to: better memory, better focus, longer attention span, and better mood and behavior regulation.

Bottom line: when the rest of your body is healthier, your brain is healthier, too. Your brain can do the problem-solving, creative, work it needs to do, when it's getting better rest, more oxygen, and more nutrients. Your brain will also be more alert and agile when confronted with crises, when it's used to processing neurochemicals, such as adrenaline, the levels of which tend to rise during physical exertion.

Integrating Fitness into Leadership

Understanding the multifaceted nature of health, including diet and the gut biome, is crucial. Integrating this knowledge into a leadership lifestyle means recognizing the interplay between physical activity, nutritional habits, and overall wellness. Below are some key aspects to consider.

The evidence is clear: A study from the CDC highlights that reducing calorie intake is more effective for weight loss than exercise alone. Similarly, research in the BMJ underscores the significant role the gut microbiome plays in obesity, offering insights into how diet influences overall health. These findings aren't just academic; they have practical implications for leaders striving to maintain a healthy lifestyle.

Incorporating physical fitness into a leadership routine involves more than just exercise. It's essential to understand the multifaceted nature of health and wellness, which includes diet, nutrition, and even understanding such things as the role of the gut biome in overall wellness.

Drawing from authoritative sources, here are key insights into diet and nutrition's role in maintaining a healthy lifestyle.

- Diet and Nutrition's Role in Weight Management: No amount of exercise can compensate for poor diet and nutrition. Research highlights the importance of reducing overall calorie intake for substantial weight loss.[38] A balanced diet, as recommended by the CDC, includes a variety of fruits, vegetables, whole grains, healthy fats, and protein sources.[39]

- Understanding Your Gut Biome: Recent studies indicate that the gut microbiome composition can predict obesity likelihood.[40] A gut rich in healthy bacteria may reduce the risk of diseases like obesity and colon cancer.[41]

- Supporting Your Body Through Proper Diet: Consuming prebiotics/fiber and probiotics/fermented foods promotes a healthy gut microbiome, aiding in disease prevention and weight management.[42]

- The Role of Exercise: While exercise is not a panacea, especially for weight-related issues, it plays a crucial role in stabilizing weight and maintaining overall health. It increases metabolism and helps maintain muscle mass, which in turn keeps metabolism higher.[43]

- Continuous Improvement and Balance: It's vital to balance calorie intake with expenditure and focus on both diet and exercise for effective weight management. This approach aligns with the leadership principle of continuous improvement, emphasizing balanced and sustainable health practices.

Additionally, I want to recognize that, for leaders with demanding schedules, integrating physical fitness can seem daunting. Here are some practical steps (pardon the pun):

- Prioritize Short, Efficient Workouts: Consider high-intensity interval training (HIIT) which can deliver effective results in shorter timeframes.

- Incorporate Movement into Daily Routine: Opt for stairs over elevators, conduct walking meetings, or use a standing desk.

- Set Realistic Goals: Start with achievable targets, such as a 15-minute daily walk, gradually increasing intensity and duration.

- Delegate to Create Time: Effective delegation of tasks can free up time, allowing for regular exercise without compromising professional responsibilities.

- Lead by Example: Use your commitment to fitness as a tool to inspire your team, integrating wellness into the organizational culture.

Let 'Em See You Sweat

In the mid 1980s, the Gillette Company launched a memorable series of TV ads for its Dry Idea antiperspirants, introducing what would become one of the most famous slogans of all time. These commercials featured various celebrities who each stated three 'never's' for their profession, and always ended with "never let 'em see you sweat." I'd like to update this wisdom for the 21st century.

Let 'em see you sweat.

Only, don't let them see you sweat due to fear or anxiety or discomfort. Let them see you sweat, because you are working hard, getting stuff done, delivering results, and passionate about high performance.

When people don't realize how much effort, sacrifice, time, and heart you poured into getting amazing results, they won't place an appropriate value on those results. So, **let them see you sweat**. Let people see what it took to get the job done, because then they will know why you're worth what they're paying you.

Before and After

When starting a personal or professional project, it's important to record your starting point. Just like weight loss ads show "before" and "after" pictures, take note of your progress by taking 'after' snapshots along the way. Don't wait for a big goal to celebrate progress, and don't stop your efforts when you see progress.

Consider the journey of a dedicated bodybuilder: consistent effort over time, documented through progress snapshots, exemplifies the continuous improvement ethos in fitness and leadership. Watching their progress is fascinating. The thing that has inspires me the most is that even though their initial transformation, when they go from "in reasonably good shape" to "bodybuilder fit," is often remarkable, you can still see their results as they continue to fine-tune their fitness regimen over time. This mirrors the leadership journey: continuous, step-by-step improvement.

I like the sandwich franchise, Jimmy John's. On their walls, they have a lot of slogans, posters, and cheeky printed material. My favorite slogan, which I have seen in every Jimmy John's, reads:

"The gap between **more** and **enough** never closes."

Leadership involves guiding your team towards *improvement, not perfection*.
Continuously compare current progress to previous results, instead of some unattainable ideal. This mindset of continuous improvement can be applied to both personal health and organizational health, with the goal being to improve, not reach perfection.

As a leader, it's essential to make a consistent effort towards improvement and not make excuses for not doing so.

KEY TAKEAWAYS

- There is a strong correlation between physical fitness and leadership effectiveness. People tend to associate good leadership with physical fitness, and research shows that physically fit leaders are perceived more positively.
- Physical fitness not only improves your health but also enhances your professional life. It increases energy, focus, passion, and creativity, making each hour of work more productive.
- Regular physical activity improves brain health, leading to increased mental energy levels, sharper focus, and more natural inspiration. This results in better connections with others and more enjoyable interactions.
- The mindset of continuous improvement is crucial in leadership. Leaders should guide their teams towards improvement, not perfection, and this mindset can be applied to both personal health and organizational health.

ACTION ITEMS

- Reflect on your physical fitness and how it may be impacting your leadership effectiveness. Consider ways you can improve your physical health.
- Incorporate regular physical activity into your routine. This could be anything from a daily walk to a rigorous workout regimen.
- Use your physical fitness journey as a way to demonstrate your commitment to hard work and high performance. Let others see your effort and progress.
- Regularly track your progress in your physical fitness journey. Take "after" snapshots along the way and celebrate your progress.
- Apply the mindset of continuous improvement to your leadership style. Continuously compare current progress to previous results, and aim for improvement rather than perfection.
- Encourage your team to also prioritize their physical health. This can lead to overall improved performance and productivity in the workplace.

CHAPTER 26

Conscientious Leadership

Humility, Integrity, and other Guiding Lights

Before You Dive Into Deep Water

In this chapter, I use terms and concepts as understood in tradi-tional, orthodox Roman Catholic theology. For those not famil-iar with this framework, I encourage seeing these principles as universal truths, interpreted through a specific spiritual lens. This perspective can offer valuable insights into leadership, regardless of one's personal beliefs or religious affiliations.

That said, this chapter is about the conscience of a leader. There-fore, in the sections that follow, I present a discussion of spiritual topics and matters. Although it may not be politically correct or even palatable to many, I have presented what I sincerely and char-itably believe is the truth, according to my strongly held religious beliefs and personal conscience.

Many people may disagree with some (or all) of what I've written, here, but please remember that, as F. Scott Fitzgerald said, it's more important to be kind than to be right, and what I will share in the rest of this chapter comes from a place of deep love for humanity and for leaders, from a kind and helpful place, and from a deep well of prayerful contemplation.

Guidance for the Guiding Spirit

Eric Hoffer was a brilliant philosopher who received the Presidential Medal of Freedom in February of 1983, shortly before his death in May of that year. In his luminous first book, The True Believer, Hoffer wrote, "A movement is pioneered by men of words, materialized by fanatics, and consolidated by men of action."[44]

Here, we are concerned with the spirit common to each of these types of men, but especially the men of action, as we are discussing principles of conscience that ought to guide leaders' hearts. Of the men of action he esteemed among the best, Hoffer wrote:

"There are, of course, rare leaders ... [who] do not hesitate to harness man's hungers and fears to weld a following and make it zealous unto death in the service of a holy cause; but ... unlike [those he esteemed among the worst], they are not tempted to use the slime of frustrated souls as mortar in the building of a new world. **The self-confidence of these rare leaders is derived from and blended with their faith in humanity, for they know that no one can be honorable unless he honors mankind.**" (emphasis mine)[45]

"No one can be honorable unless he honors mankind."
-- ERIC HOFFER

To "honor mankind" is to love mankind, to speak and act with charity toward one's neighbors, as Jesus Christ taught. This is the second most important spiritual principle for leaders, after loving God, the Creator of all.

In the daily practice of leadership, living a sacramental life as a Catholic is fundamentally about bringing spiritual principles into everyday actions. This means actively seeking grace through the sacraments - like participating in the Eucharist and Reconciliation - which in turn, shapes our interactions, decisions, and the way we lead. It's about embodying these principles in our conduct, whether in the kindness we show to our colleagues, the integrity with which we handle our projects, or the mercy we extend in our professional relationships. By living a sacramental life, we bring a deeper, spiritual dimension to our leadership, making our actions not just tasks, but offerings of service aligned with our faith.

However you practice the two overarching principles of loving God and loving your neighbor as yourself, I think you will find that your authentic practice of virtue will also necessarily include at least six additional, more specifically actionable principles, which we'll discuss next.

Always Live in Integrity.

Living in integrity in leadership means more than honesty; it involves a commitment to excellence and justice in every decision and action. For example, a leader who values integrity might refuse to cut corners on a project, even under tight deadlines, prioritizing quality and ethical practices.

Integrity also compels one to be rationally compassionate, humble enough to admit that there are many things one cannot, and does not, know. Finally, Integrity motivates one to act against injustice, give voice to righteousness, and advocate for justifiable beliefs.

The story of Daniel in the lions' den exemplifies integrity. This story is found in the sixth chapter of the Old Testament Book of the Prophet Daniel. Despite facing life-threatening circumstances, Daniel maintained his integrity, staying true to his principles and faith. His unwavering commitment under immense pressure serves as a profound example for leaders: to maintain honesty and ethical standards, even when it's challenging. It teaches us that true leadership is about sticking to one's core values, regardless of the consequences. Daniel's story can serve as an inspiration for leaders to uphold integrity even in the face of challenges.

While living in integrity forms the foundation, avoiding expectations is another crucial aspect of leadership. This principle helps in managing desires and maintaining emotional balance.

Avoid Expectations.

Completely eliminating expectations is one of those goals which serves as something to aim at, but which is not really practically possible. Avoiding expectations, however, is.

Expectations arise from cycles of desire and attachment, leading to suffering when we become attached to desires which remain un-fulfilled. Our desires, per se, are not the source of our suffering, but our attachments to those desires are.

Avoiding expectations short-circuits the process of becoming attached to our desires. If we desire something, but refrain from expecting what we desire, then we do not become attached, and if the desire fails to be fulfilled, we are not disappointed, we suffer no feeling of loss, and our inner peace remains undisturbed.

Free yourself from the tyranny of expectations.[46] Building on the theme of inner peace and emotional regulation, humility stands as a cornerstone of virtuous leadership.

Be Humble.

Humility is the gateway to all virtue, the antithesis of that first and greatest of all sins—pride.

"The sin of pride is a heart attitude expressed in an unhealthy, exaggerated attention to self and an elevated view of one's abilities, accomplishments, position, or possessions. Pride has been called 'the cancer of the soul,' 'the beginning of all sin,' and 'sin in its final form.' Ten Hebrew words and two Greek words are generally used in the Bible to refer to it. Pride, in its sinful form, is the direct opposite of humility, a trait that is highly praised and rewarded by God."[47]

Humility is also the foundation of prayer, that is, of spiritual intercourse with God.[48] If you would be virtuous, first be humble.

The parable of the Good Samaritan, found in the Gospel According to St. Luke, chapter 10, verses 25-37, is a powerful illustration of mercy and humility. It tells the story of a man who, unlike others, stops to help a stranger in need, crossing cultural and social boundaries to do so. This narrative encourages leaders to act with compassion and humility, to see beyond societal divisions, and to extend help and understanding, especially to those who are often overlooked or marginalized. It's a reminder that as leaders, our actions should be guided by compassion and a genuine desire to uplift others.

Be Merciful.

The Jubilee of Mercy was an Extraordinary Holy Year that commenced on December 8, 2015 (the Solemnity of the Immaculate Conception) and closed on November 20, 2016 (the Solemnity of Christ the King). During the Jubilee Year of Mercy was the time when, as a recent convert to the Holy Roman Catholic faith, I first deeply explored the Spiritual Works of Mercy and the Corporal Works of Mercy.

In brief, the Spiritual Works of Mercy are:

- Counseling the doubtful,

- Instructing the ignorant,

- Admonishing the sinner,

- Comforting the sorrowful,

- Forgiving injuries,

- Bearing wrongs patiently, and

- Praying for the living and the dead.

In brief, the Corporal Works of Mercy are:

- Feed the hungry,

- Give drink to the thirsty,

- Shelter the homeless,

- Visit the sick,

- Visit the prisoners,

- Bury the dead, and

- Give alms to the poor.

I love what Fr. Wade Menezes said upon the closing of the Extraordinary Jubilee Year of Mercy:

"...[Mercy] is Who God is. It's love's second name. God is more interested in our future than in our past. He's more interested in the kind of person we can yet become, than in the kind of person we used to be. While indeed taking our sins seriously – no doubt – whether mortal or venial (because they have in someway severed or wounded our super-natural relationship with Him), God *never*, *ever* takes those sins as the last word. Why? Because He knows He's made us in His image and likeness, He knows He calls us *constantly* to Himself to live a life of Sanctifying Grace, and He knows He is our God."[49]

In the *Compendium of the Catechism of the Catholic Church*, #391 poses this question: "What does the acceptance of God's mercy require form us?" The answer: "It requires that we admit our faults and repent of our sins. God Himself by His word and His Spirit lays bare our sins and gives us the truth of conscience and the hope of forgiveness."

Mercy, my friends, is the disposition to be kind and forgiving – a disposition we no doubt want God to practice toward us. Founded on compassion, mercy is the ready willingness to help anyone in need, especially those in need of pardon or reconciliation. *Now*, if *we* want to receive this great gift from God, we have to be willing to give it to *others*..."

Indeed, in the Gospel According to St. Matthew, Jesus taught:

"For if you forgive men their trespasses, your heavenly Father also will forgive you; but if you do not forgive men their trespasses, neither will your Father forgive your trespasses."[50]

Our capacity to receive mercy from God depends on our capacity to show mercy to others.

Mercy in leadership translates to practices like giving second chances to team members who falter, offering support instead of immediate censure, and understanding the human aspects behind professional mistakes.

Cultivate Fortitude.

Spiritual fortitude, or the stalwart practice of courage, is not just a religious concept but a universal virtue, essential in overcoming challenges and adversity in leadership. Fortitude manifests variously as forbearance (of wrongs, of unpleasant circumstances, of suffering); strength, especially in adversity; endurance; and anti-fragility or resilience when confronted with uncertertainty.

Cultivating spiritual fortitude in a leadership role involves resilience and perseverance. When facing a challenging project or a crisis, a leader with fortitude stays committed to the goal, maintaining a calm and steady approach, and inspiring the team through personal example.

"Fortitude is the moral virtue that ensures firmness in difficulties and constancy in the pursuit of the good. It strengthens the resolve to resist temptations and to overcome obstacles in the moral life. The virtue of fortitude enables one to conquer fear, even fear of death, and to face trials and persecutions. It disposes one even to renounce and sacrifice his life in defense of a just cause. 'The Lord is my strength and my song.' 'In the world you have tribulation; but be of good cheer, I have overcome the world.'"[51]

If you would develop the virtue of fortitude, practice patience and strive with hope for greatness, for God's glory not your own. Fortitude is heroic, the hallmark of a powerful leader.

Love Wisdom.

If you've never fallen in love, nothing I could say, here, would make any sense to you.

The best I can do is point you to a book. I recommend reading *Falling in Love with Wisdom: American Philosophers Talk About Their Calling*. This book is a collection of over 60 philosophers' memoirs recalling how they fell in love with wisdom. Philosophy is the love of wisdom.

Growing up, I was required to memorize a lot of Bible verses, and, each morning, we would read from the book of Proverbs on the way to school. I'm not sure what it says about me, but Proverbs 29:3 has always put a smile on my face. It says: "He who loves wisdom makes his father glad, but one who keeps company with harlots squanders his substance."

Given the salacious content of the latter half of this verse, I've always interpreted the word "love," as used in the first half of the verse, in a very sensual way. The way the author of Proverbs uses "love," here seems to suggest a very vigorous and productive love. It's the kind of love that one might have for their spouse.

In fact, in the book of Wisdom, the author describes King Solomon's love for Wisdom in precisely this way:

"I loved her and sought her from my youth, and I desired to take her for my bride, and I became enamored of her beauty."[52]

Earlier in that same book, the author writes: "... for God loves nothing so much as the man who lives with wisdom."

In Psalm 111:10 (RSVCE), we read: "The fear of the Lord is the beginning of wisdom; a good understanding have all those who practice it. His praise endures for ever."

This is echoed in Proverbs 9:10: "The fear of the Lord is the beginning of wisdom, and the knowledge of the Holy One is insight."

This "fear" the psalmist and the author of Proverbs describes is more akin to wonder or amazement.

Even Socrates wrote, "Wisdom begins in wonder."

Have a love affair with wisdom. Fall in love with wisdom. Marry wisdom. Wisdom will never betray you. True wisdom will always bring you closer to your Creator, the Divine Source of all that is good. That's the kind of supportive, loving spouse every leader needs. The spirit of a leader is nurtured through a commitment to these timeless principles. By integrating integrity, humility, mercy, fortitude, and wisdom into our leadership, we not only elevate our own character but also positively impact those we lead.

KEY TAKEAWAYS

- Spiritual Foundation in Leadership: Embracing virtues like integrity, mercy, humility, and wisdom, rooted in a deep love for humanity and God, is fundamental to effective leadership.
- Integrity Through Actions and Decisions: Upholding honesty, ethical practices, and compassion in every action and decision is key to maintaining integrity as a leader.
- Emotional Balance through Avoiding Expectations: Practicing detachment from expectations helps maintain inner peace, allowing leaders to respond to challenges with clarity and focus.
- Humility Is the Gateway to Virtue: Embracing humility paves the way for genuine leadership, fostering a spirit of service and openness to learning from others.
- Mercy in Leadership: Showing mercy, understanding, and forgiveness in leadership cultivates a supportive and compassionate work environment.
- Cultivating Courage and Wisdom: Developing fortitude to face challenges and a love for wisdom guides leaders towards making informed, ethical, and empathetic decisions.

ACTION ITEMS

- Reflect on Virtues: Regularly assess how well you are embodying virtues like integrity, humility, and mercy in your leadership.
- Integrate Spiritual Practices: Incorporate spiritual practices into your daily routine to strengthen your virtues and leadership qualities.
- Practice Detachment: Work on detaching from rigid expectations to enhance emotional resilience and adaptability.
- Foster Humility and Mercy: Actively seek opportunities to demonstrate humility and mercy in your interactions with team members and colleagues.
- Embrace Challenges with Fortitude: Approach challenging situations with courage and perseverance, using them as opportunities for growth and leadership development.
- Pursue Wisdom: Engage in continuous learning and reflection to deepen your understanding and love of wisdom.

CHAPTER 27

The Strategic Pause

Rest as a Leadership Tool

As leaders in a fast-paced world, we often forget the power of stepping back and taking a break. My personal journey to understanding this came unexpectedly, during a family event that turned into a lesson on the importance of rest in leadership.

Not long after I started my law practice and started to build momentum as a new business owner, my sister-in-law and her then-fiancée decided to get married in St. Lucia, a romantic Caribbean island with fantastic views, beautiful villas, gorgeous beaches, and endless activities for tourists—an island paradise.

Instead of being grateful for an all-expenses-paid vacation to an island I'd always wanted to visit, at first, I was frustratingly focused on how I was going to run my business from 2,200+ miles away! In hindsight, I look back at how I initially thought and felt about the destination wedding, and I feel shame and regret.

After making too much fuss over whether or not there was Wi-Fi in the picturesque cliff-top villa where we stayed, eventually, I relaxed and decided my clients and the attendees at the speaking engagement I had to miss would just have to understand. I had to force myself to shift my focus—something that, at the time, I was terrible at doing.

After all, I decided, family matters more than anything else. The trip was amazing! I had a wonderful time, and I only regret that I didn't just completely leave all my work and devices behind, set an auto-responder on my e-mail, and forget about practicing law and running the firm for a week.

As leaders, it can be challenging to prioritize rest and leisure time. However, taking breaks and going on vacations are not only important for our well-being and the well-being of our families, but they can also benefit our businesses in the long run.

In this chapter, we will explore the benefits of taking time away from work and offer practical advice for leaders who struggle to slow down.

"Slow is smooth; smooth is fast."

THE SLOW WAY IS THE FAST WAY

Leaders who are dedicated to their work and the success of their businesses often find it difficult to take time off. But it is essential to remember that taking breaks and going on vacations is an obligation to yourself, your family, and your business.

When you slow down and take time off, everything you do will go more smoothly.

As the Zen proverb says, "The slow way is the fast way." This is also reflected in the Marines' saying, "Slow is smooth; smooth is fast." Taking time off allows you to avoid burnout and complete tasks, projects, and long-term goals in a more timely manner.

Consider the practices of renowned leaders like Bill Gates and Steve Jobs. Bill Gates is known for taking two one-week retreats each year to a secluded cabin, where he disconnects from technology to read and ponder the future of his endeavors.[53] Similarly, Steve Jobs was famous for his long walks and meditation sessions, using these times away from the digital world to clear his mind and generate innovative ideas.[54] These examples showcase how stepping away from daily routines and technology can foster creativity and strategic thinking, rejuvenating a leader's vision and approach.

GRANTING PERSPECTIVE THROUGH DISTANCE

Taking a break from your day-to-day operations and stepping back from your business can be challenging at first, but distance can be a gift. It forces you to delegate, delay, or refuse certain activities and helps put into perspective which of your business operations are truly necessary.

When you're out of the office, consider what most concerns you. Are you managing a new employee or trying to sign a new client? What can you delay or delegate to someone else?

Effective delegation, by the way, is not just about offloading tasks; it's about empowering your team and building trust. By entrusting responsibilities to your team members, you not only foster their growth but also create space for your own rest and rejuvenation.

This raises important questions about your business operations, such as whether your family, organization, business, or community has effective policies and procedures in place to ensure everything runs smoothly while you're away.

IT'S JUST A BREAK, NOT A BREAK-UP

Remember, you're not leaving forever. Even a week away can seem like an eternity in the fast-paced world of business, but it's just a break.

Consider working with a temporary assistant to help you stay connected and handle calls, emails, and other mundane tasks. Consider drafting a written contract to govern your relationship with the assistant and provide them with instructions for handling emergencies.

Additionally, don't rely too much on the internet, as it can be unreliable and pose security and financial challenges for remote work. Instead, have a plan, prioritize, and enjoy your time off.

Just like God rested after creating everything, it's important for leaders to follow His example and give themselves a break. It's good for the soul and for your family or team.

As we've explored through personal insights and broader perspectives, the value of rest in leadership cannot be overstated. Oh, yeah... And don't forget to pack sunscreen!

KEY TAKEAWAYS

- Embracing Rest as a Leadership Strategy: Regular rest and leisure are not just personal benefits but strategic leadership practices that enhance overall effectiveness and well-being.
- Efficiency through Slowing Down: The principle of "Slow is smooth; smooth is fast" highlights the productivity gains from taking breaks, preventing burnout, and ultimately enhancing efficiency.
- Gaining Perspective from Distance: Stepping away from daily operations provides critical perspective, enabling leaders to focus on essential tasks and streamline business processes.
- Temporary Disconnection for Long-term Benefits: Short breaks are necessary for long-term sustainability in leadership. They offer mental rejuvenation and prevent burnout.
- Rest as a Spiritual and Mental Practice: Following the biblical example of rest, leaders can find balance and renewal, benefiting their spiritual and mental health.

ACTION ITEMS

- Plan for Regular Breaks: Schedule downtime, ensuring you regularly step away from work to rejuvenate and gain perspective.
- Apply Efficiency Principles: Reflect on how taking breaks can streamline your leadership approach and improve efficiency.
- Delegate Effectively: Develop a delegation plan to manage responsibilities during your absence, ensuring business continuity.
- Communicate and Set Boundaries: Clearly communicate your availability during breaks to your team and set boundaries to ensure you can fully disconnect.
- Reflect and Rejuvenate: Use your time off for personal growth, relaxation, and mental rejuvenation, away from the pressures of leadership.
- Evaluate Post-Break Impact: After returning, assess the impact of your break on your leadership effectiveness and make adjustments as needed.

CHAPTER 28

Unifying Diverse Minds

The Art of Team Synergy

Building a team is a challenging but crucial aspect of leadership success. No one can achieve greatness on their own, and every effective leader understands the importance of creating a strong and cohesive team. To build a great team, it is essential to have a deep understanding of team-building principles and practices.

One of the books that has made a significant impact on my understanding of team-building is *Lead Together: The Bold, Brave, Intentional Path to Scaling Your Business* by Brent Lowe, Susan Basterfield, and Travis Marsh. This book resonates with me and offers valuable insights for leaders, regardless of whether you prefer a self-managing organization structure or a more traditional, hierarchical team. If you're interested in working in a collaborative leadership setting, the insights in this book will be even more beneficial to you.

Another book that provides useful insights on team-building is *Zero to One: Notes on Startups, or How to Build the Future* by Peter

Thiel. Thiel suggests that when it comes to hiring, it's essential to consider the perspective of the candidate. Every company promises competitive salaries, working with intelligent people, and attractive perks.

However, these factors alone are not enough to attract the best talent. To stand out, leaders must communicate the unique and important aspects of their company or team and explain why it is meaningful, valuable, and purposeful.

To incentivize employees, it's essential to provide a stable income and a generous bonus structure tied to performance. The salary and benefits should be comparable to the industry standard, but bonuses should be substantial enough to place total compensation above the 75th percentile. To encourage high performance, it's crucial to make the requirements for earning bonuses clear, measurable, and fair.

> **"Incentives Matter."**
> -- DR. JAMES GWARTNEY, ET AL.,
> *COMMON SENSE ECONOMICS*

Diversity or D.I.E.

When it comes to building a high-performing team, it's crucial to strive for cohesiveness and shared values among team members. While diversity is often seen as a strength, it's important to focus on the types of diversity that will drive success for your team.

Your team members should share a core perspective and approach, even if they come from different backgrounds and hold different opinions. This commonality will make them stand out as a unique and effective team, and will foster a sense of unity and shared purpose.

While superficial aspects of diversity are often the focus of "Diversity Equity and Inclusion" ("DEI") initiatives, an emphasis on cognitive and conative diversity will do far more to maximize the team's potential.

More Juice Per Squeeze

Building a high-performing team is essential for a successful leader. To achieve this, it's important to start with defining and communicating clear roles for each team member. This helps to reduce conflict and avoid turf wars. A well-informed team with a sense of purpose is a healthy thing, but it's equally important to ensure that the team's approach is based on education and rationality rather than blind devotion.

It's also crucial to have clarity on who is responsible for what and how much authority each person has in decision-making. This can be achieved through good governing documents, which should be in place from the early stages of a business.

Lastly, don't overlook the importance of training and onboarding each team member. This is not just a formality, but a vital rite of passage for building a strong and cohesive team. Even the best governing documents won't solve everything, so make sure your onboarding process is effective and thorough.

As an attorney, I have had a lot of experience resolving issues with dysfunctional corporate leadership. In my experience, the most dysfunctional teams have a lack of leadership and a lot of control-seeking behavior.

I've seen cases where a minority member in a limited liability company, who held only 4% of the membership interests in the company, acted like they owned the entire company. I've seen others teams in which decision-making was paralyzed due to disagreements between equal partners.

Good team governance and clear roles are key to avoiding these issues and ensuring a high-performing team.

Building a cohesive U.N.I.T.

Each team-building process tends to follow four discrete stages, which are easy to remember when one uses the acronym "**U.N.I.T.**"

"**U**" stands for "unify." Determine what roles duties and authority will be assigned to each member of the team, ensuring that the group can act as a single unified entity. Remember, your collective thinking is shifting from many (individuals) to one (team).

"**N**" stands for "nudge." Inspiring and supporting good communication and building up relationships between team members, whenever possible, should be done with gentle nudges. Respect boundaries and foster safe secure attachments.

"**I**" stands for "include." In your team build a culture of inclusivity. Prioritize cooperation over competition. Encourage everyone to acknowledge other's contributions as well as remain accountable for their own.

"**T**" stands for "tally." Gauge the collective progress your team makes towards shared goals at regular intervals, celebrating wins and raising awareness around lapses in performance.

Following the principles described in the "U.N.I.T." acronym, will keep you on track as you build your team.

Building a great team requires ongoing learning and growth as a leader. This chapter is meant to be a starting point, not an ending point, in your journey to build a deep understanding of team building. So, continue to seek out and learn from other great resources on the subject.

While the 'U.N.I.T.' framework lays a solid foundation for team building, it's also crucial to navigate the complexities and challenges inherent in this process.

Overcoming Team-Building Challenges

Building a team is akin to navigating a complex labyrinth; it's fraught with challenges that can test even the most seasoned leader. Here, we delve into some common obstacles in team building and explore how to adeptly navigate through them.

Embracing diversity in your team is like adding different spices to a dish - it can enhance the flavor but also leads to the risk of conflicting tastes. When divergent viewpoints lead to conflict, the key lies in fostering an environment of open dialogue and respect.

Encourage your team to embrace differences as opportunities for growth and learning. Remember, resolving conflicts isn't about winning an argument; it's about harmonizing different chords to create a beautiful symphony.

Change is often met with resistance, like a boat struggling against the current. To ease this resistance, involve your team in the change process. Make them co-navigators in your journey. Explain the 'why' behind changes and provide the necessary training and resources to help them adapt. When people feel part of the change, they're more likely to row in sync with you.

Ineffective communication can create chasms within a team. To bridge these gaps, establish clear channels of communication. Regular team meetings, open feedback sessions, and encouraging active listening can turn these chasms into stepping stones for better understanding and collaboration.

Unclear roles can lead to a chaotic orchestra where everyone is playing a different tune. Clarify each team member's role and responsibilities as if you're a conductor ensuring every musician knows their part in the symphony. Regular reviews of these roles can keep the music harmonious and aligned with your team's objectives.

Cultivating Trust and Cohesion

A team without trust is like a tree without roots - it can't stand strong. Foster trust through transparency and reliability. Team-building activities that promote mutual understanding can strengthen these roots, creating a team that stands tall and united.

As a leader, you're the captain of your ship. Ineffective leadership can steer the team off course. Commit to your growth as a leader. Be open to feedback, lead by example, and prioritize the development and well-being of your crew.

Over-relying on top performers is like overloading one side of a boat - it risks capsizing. Distribute tasks evenly, recognize and nurture the potential in all team members, and create opportunities for everyone to shine. This balance can prevent burnout and foster a sense of equity and belonging in the team.

Incorporating these strategies into your team-building process can transform obstacles into stepping stones towards creating a cohesive and high-performing team. Remember, the path to a successful team is not always smooth, but with the right approach, every challenge can be an opportunity to grow stronger together.

Finally, please, exercise caution when selecting and integrating members into your team! Your team is unique and special, and its singularity can be both a strength and a weakness. To maximize its strength, pay close attention to the unique needs of your team and avoid expecting them to conform to a poorly communicated normative standard.

KEY TAKEAWAYS

- Essentiality of Team Building in Leadership: Understanding and applying team-building principles is key to forming strong, cohesive teams, which are foundational to leadership success.
- Effective Talent Attraction: Communicating the distinctiveness and purpose of your organization is crucial in attracting and retaining top talent.
- Importance of Diverse Perspectives: Focus on diversity in thoughts and problem-solving approaches, ensuring the team shares core values and goals.
- Structural Clarity and Training: Clear role definition, comprehensive governing documents, and an effective onboarding process are vital components of successful team building.
- U.N.I.T. Framework Application: Utilize the U.N.I.T. framework (Unify, Nudge, Include, Tally) to guide the team-building process, ensuring a cohesive and effective team.

ACTION ITEMS

- Enhance Communication: Develop strategies to clearly communicate your team's uniqueness and purpose to potential recruits.
- Diversity Assessment: Regularly assess your team's diversity in cognitive and conative aspects, and identify areas for improvement.
- Role Clarity and Governance Review: Conduct periodic reviews of team roles and governing documents for clarity and effectiveness.
- Optimize Onboarding: Evaluate and enhance your onboarding process to ensure it effectively integrates new members into the team.
- Implement U.N.I.T. Framework: Apply the U.N.I.T. framework in your team-building efforts, regularly assessing each aspect for continuous improvement.

CHAPTER 29

Mastering Meetings

The Leader's Guide to Effective Conferencing

Imagine stepping into a meeting room, knowing that the next hour could pivotally steer the direction of your entire project. In the dynamic realm of leadership, meetings are far more than mere entries in our calendars. They are crucibles where ideas clash and meld, shaping the future of our teams and endeavors. Yet, all too often, meetings become mired in a quagmire of inefficiency, leaving trails of confusion and missed opportunities. This chapter is dedicated to elevating the mundane meeting to a strategic tool in your leadership arsenal, transforming each gathering into a wellspring of purpose, efficiency, and impactful outcomes.

Many of the recommendations made in this book have included or involved cooperation, collaboration, or consultation with others. By now, you should understand that, while it may sometimes feel "lonely at the top," leadership is not a one-person activity. Even if you're not planning to go full-on Lead Together a la Brent Lowe, et al., you're going to need the support of an amazing team if you're going to be an effective leader.

How do you get the most out of each meeting with your team, or a member of your team, though? What about other meetings—such as with clients, vendors, stakeholders, or others? Meetings are vital to your leadership efforts, but a study of 19 million meetings and interviews with more than 6.500 working professionals in the U.S., U.K., and Germany concluded that, in 2019, "the cost of poorly organized meetings" was around "$399 billion in the U.S. and $58 billion in the U.K."[55]

> **"When leaders know how to lead great meetings, there's less time wasted and less frustration. We have more energy to do the work that matters, realize our full potential, and do great things."**
> -- JUSTIN ROSENSTEIN

In the survey, respondents most often reported:

- "Poorly organized meetings mean I don't have enough time to do the rest of my work (44%);"
- "Unclear actions lead to confusion (43%);"
- Bad organization results in a loss of focus on projects (38%);"
- "Irrelevant attendees slow progress (31%t);" and
- "Inefficient processes weaken client/supplier relationships (26%)."

Good leaders will boost productivity and morale (and protect valuable resources) by improving the quality of their meetings. The rest of this brief chapter outlines how to do just that!

Five Essentials for Optimal Meetings

1. **Check Your Impulse**. Imagine before scheduling a team meeting, a project manager reflects on the agenda and realizes that the updates can be efficiently communicated via email. By resisting the urge to call a meeting, she saves everyone's time and keeps the team focused on their tasks.

   Ask yourself, "Is this meeting really necessary, or would asynchronous communication work?" For the purposes of this chapter, I include phone calls, especially conference calls, within the definition of a "meeting," because it requires a person to dedicate so much time and focus to the activity that other tasks tend to be excluded (if they're participating to the degree intended by the organizer).

   Asynchronous communication (i.e., exchanging information, but not in real time) can include pre-recorded video messages (e.g., Loom, etc.), e-mail, instant messaging (e.g., Slack, Teams, etc.), or even an old-fashioned Memorandum.

   Never schedule a meeting when an e-mail will do. Likewise, never include more people in the meeting than are necessary. Establish the type of meeting, decide how it will flow, and set a maximum time for the meeting in advance; then stick to it.

2. **Schedule**. A department head utilizes Calendly to schedule a crucial strategy meeting. This tool aligns everyone's availability without the back-and-forth emails, ensuring a smooth scheduling process and higher attendance.

In my personal experience, this is one of the most painful parts of meetings. Scheduling (and rescheduling) meetings is a huge pain in the neck! Using automated tools, such as Calendly, can help. Carefully selecting your meeting date and time can make a huge difference in how the meeting flows.

3. **Have and Use a Pre-printed Agenda**. In a weekly team meeting, the leader distributes a well-structured agenda in advance. This clarity guides the discussion, ensuring all topics are covered efficiently, and the meeting concludes within the allocated time. There are some excellent meeting agenda templates available online. Which one you use is less important than the fact that you're using one! Something is better than nothing. Revise and improve your meeting agenda templates until they work well for your team. Make sure everyone receives an agenda ahead of the meeting.

4. **Be Present**. During a project debrief, the team leader actively listens to feedback, encourages open discussion, and ensures each member's voice is heard, leading to more in-depth insights and a sense of shared ownership among the team.

   Keep discussion focused and relevant. Ask thoughtful questions. Allow people to disagree in constructive ways. Actively listen. Take good notes. In short, allow meetings to be useful discussions. Make sure everyone has a chance (and feels emotionally safe) to authentically contribute to the discussion.

   There is no need for a person to attend a meeting if they can't participate. If someone cannot participate, they may as well receive a written summary of the Meeting Notes. Spending time in the meeting is just a waste of time for non-participants.

5. **Solicit Feedback**. After a cross-departmental meeting, the manager sends out a feedback survey to all participants. The responses reveal insights into the meeting's effectiveness and areas for improvement, leading to enhanced future meetings.

Go over the minutes of the meeting with key stakeholders. Send out a request to all attendees, surveying them about the meeting and inviting feedback that they didn't have either the time or the presence of mind to provide in the meeting.

Your team's meeting "Meeting M.O." will be unique to them. Justin Rosenstein said, "When leaders know how to lead great meetings, there's less time wasted and less frustration. We have more energy to do the work that matters, realize our full potential, and do great things."[56] Your job, as a leader, is to ensure meetings move the action forward and everyone has a voice. Meetings should never hold you back. They should never cost you money. On the contrary, they should be among your most productive activities. It's up to you to make that happen.

Mastering the art of effective meetings is a hallmark of exceptional leadership, distinguishing those who merely manage from those who truly inspire and direct their teams. The insights and strategies we've explored here are your tools to turn every meeting from a mundane routine into a dynamic force for progress and innovation. Remember, each meeting is a stage where you can inspire, unite, and drive your team towards remarkable achievements. Let's harness this opportunity and make every moment count for our teams and our goals.

KEY TAKEAWAYS

- Strategic Significance of Meetings: Understand that meetings are not just routine gatherings but crucial strategic tools that can significantly impact projects and team dynamics.
- Efficiency through Asynchronous Communication: Recognize the value of asynchronous communication to improve efficiency, and avoid unnecessary meetings.
- Effective Scheduling Tools: Utilize tools like Calendly for smooth scheduling, enhancing meeting attendance and flow.
- The Importance of a Structured Agenda: Implement a well-structured agenda for every meeting to ensure focus and productivity.
- Active Participation and Presence: Emphasize the need for active listening, constructive disagreement, and full participation in meetings for optimal outcomes.
- Continuous Improvement Through Feedback: Regularly solicit feedback post-meeting to continually enhance the meeting quality and effectiveness.

ACTION ITEMS

- Reflect on Meeting Necessity: Before scheduling a meeting, critically assess if the matter could be more efficiently addressed asynchronously.
- Leverage Scheduling Technology: Employ scheduling tools to streamline the meeting planning process and ensure optimal timing for all participants.
- Agenda Development: Create and regularly update a meeting agenda template that suits your team's needs, and distribute it in advance of meetings.
- Foster Engagement and Participation: During meetings, practice and promote active engagement, allowing room for diverse opinions and constructive dialogue.
- Post-Meeting Feedback: Implement a system to collect and review feedback from meeting attendees to identify areas for improvement.
- Apply Insights to Future Meetings: Use insights from each meeting to refine your approach and enhance the effectiveness of future gatherings.

CHAPTER 30

Time and Leadership

Prioritizing for Peak Performance

Spending more time on a task does not mean you're doing better work or that the task is more important. Using more resources —whether money, time, effort, or some other resource—when one could use fewer resources to accomplish an equally valuable result is wasteful.

Of all the resources at your disposal, time may be the most valuable. A good leader will avoid wasting others' time as well as their own. In this brief chapter, you will find principles and tips for reclaiming your time and using it to be more effective and more efficient in your leadership efforts.

> **"If you don't prioritize your life, someone else will."**
> -- GREG MCKEOWN

The art of mastering your schedule is simply the art of mastering your priorities. As Greg McKeown has said, "If you don't prioritize your life, someone else will."[57]

No one else can tell you *what* to prioritize, in your life, because your priorities must flow from your own personal values and must reflect your dynamic circumstances. Here, however, are some insights for *how* to prioritize your life.

Time Management Is A Waste of Time

Books like *The 4-Hour Workweek*, by Timothy Ferriss, and *Essentialism*, by Greg McKeown, are essential reading for any leader serious about mastering his schedule. My recommendation is that one read both of these excellent books. At the risk of being a little redundant, however, I want to highlight some common themes appearing in these valuable works, adding some of my own ideas on time management.

The first thing you should do when approaching the concept of time management is forget about it. This suggestion comes from Tim Ferriss, in *The 4-Hour Workweek*. I just happen to agree. It's not enough, however, to simply eliminate something. The human mind, like nature, abhors a vacuum. So, you need to replace time management with something else—in this case, priority management.

The work of mastering your schedule, primarily, is the work of managing priorities and setting and communicating expectations regarding them. Delegation, too, is an essential and powerful time-saver.

When you know how to prioritize your work and your focus, you will spend your time on what is most important, rather than wasting time on low-priority things.

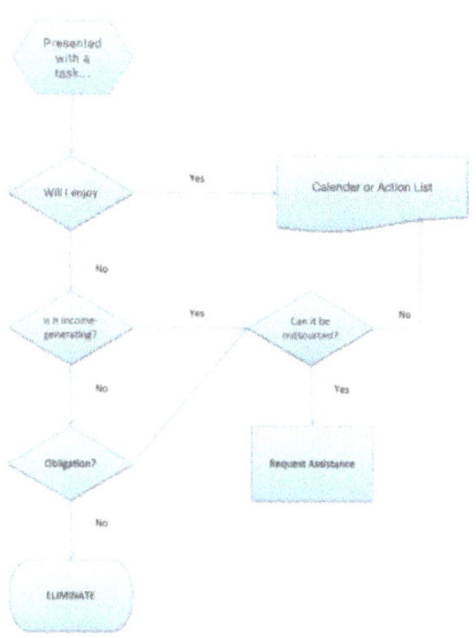

Easy Delegation Example for Busy Professionals

To help you surface your priorities, here are five considerations for optimizing your priorities or your priority stack. These are presented in no particular order.

7 Ideas that Should Shape Your Priorities

The Endowment Effect. The endowment effect is the tendency to value something more because it is already owned or has been given to us. This bias can lead to poor decision-making, such as continuing to do something simply because it has been done before. Cognitive biases, like the endowment effect, are common to everyone. Recognizing and compensating for these biases can improve critical thinking and decision-making.

The Pareto Principle. The Pareto Principle, also known as the 80/20 rule, states that 80% of outcomes come from 20% of causes. For example, 20% of customers may generate 80% of revenues or complaints. To maximize the impact of resources, focus on the 20% of causes that generate 80% of desirable effects and consider the other 80% disposable. This process can be repeated to improve results.

The Planning Fallacy. The planning fallacy is the tendency to underestimate the time, cost, and risks of a task, even when this contradicts past experience.

This bias was first identified by Kahneman and Tversky in their 1977 paper on cognitive biases. The planning fallacy arises from our tendency to ignore outside data and leads to inaccurate predictions about the future.

An example of this is the construction of the Sydney Opera House, which took longer and cost more than planned due to unforeseen difficulties.

To avoid the planning fallacy, Kahneman recommends getting an "outside view" by seeking the insight of experienced experts.

Boundaries. These are different from emotional boundaries, yet managing your priorities effectively requires you to understand your limitations and set clear boundaries with others. Communicate how much time you have available for tasks and make your priorities clear. This will prevent your time from being wasted by others. Be prepared to reallocate resources to your highest priority activities as needed.

Worry. I recently heard it said "Worry is like praying for something that you don't want to happen." My teacher and mentor Matthew Corlett has said to me, more than once, the things that will manifest in our lives are those things to which we have the strongest emotional attachment. Whatever it is that you have the strongest emotional attachment to is the thing that's most likely to show up in your life.

Worrying about something can cause it to happen, a phenomenon known as a self-fulfilling prophecy. By being afraid of or focused on something, you may behave in ways that cause it to happen. This is often referred to as the law of attraction or unintended consequences.

To avoid this, it is important to release worries and trust in a higher power. This requires humility and an understanding that you have only a limited influence on your circumstances.

Rational Ignorance. Rational ignorance is the reasonable decision to not gather more information than is necessary to make a decision. This is necessary because it is impossible to know everything. It is important to consider the cost and value of information when making a decision, especially for leaders. A good leader will understand the value of information and act accordingly, relying on trusted advisers when necessary. It is important to balance the cost and value of information and avoid both excessive ignorance and excessive knowledge.

> **"If you chase two rabbits, you will lose them both."**
> -- RUSSIAN PROVERB

Interruptions. Finally, as you pursue mastery over your schedule, make an effort to short-circuit interruptions. To avoid interruptions and achieve mastery over your schedule, stop multitasking, set boundaries and protect your focused time, begin each task with a clear goal, aim to enter a state of flow, and create an interruption reduction plan. Track interruptions to identify their sources and frequency, then take action to short-circuit the processes that lead to them. Don't judge or evaluate interruptions, as every data point is valuable.

Remember, you can't completely control your schedule, avoid or prevent every interruption, or bend time to your will.

KEY TAKEAWAYS

- Time is a valuable resource, and effective leaders avoid wasting it. Mastering your schedule is about managing priorities and setting and communicating expectations.
- The concept of time management should be replaced with priority management. This involves focusing on what is most important rather than wasting time on low-priority tasks.
- Cognitive biases, such as the endowment effect and the planning fallacy, can lead to poor decision-making. Recognizing and compensating for these biases can improve critical thinking and decision-making.
- The Pareto Principle, or the 80/20 rule, can be used to maximize the impact of resources. Focus on the 20% of causes that generate 80% of desirable effects.
- Setting clear boundaries, understanding limitations, and communicating priorities can prevent time from being wasted by others.

ACTION ITEMS

- Read books like "The 4-Hour Workweek" and "Essentialism" to gain insights on mastering your schedule and managing priorities.
- Recognize and compensate for cognitive biases, such as the endowment effect and the planning fallacy, in your decision-making process.
- Apply the Pareto Principle in your work to focus on the most impactful tasks.
- Set clear boundaries and communicate your priorities to others to prevent your time from being wasted.
- Track interruptions to identify their sources and frequency, then take action to short-circuit the processes that lead to them. This will help you protect your focused time and achieve mastery over your schedule.

CHAPTER 31

Little Wins, Major Gains

The Art of Building Momentum

In 2020-2021, I participated in Dent Global's Key Person of Influence ("KPI") program, which has been dubbed "The world's leading personal brand accelerator" by the Huffington Post and "One of the top business growth accelerators in the world" by Entrepreneur.com. The lessons I learned in the KPI program were amazing, and I made some incredible friends, too. One of the things we did throughout the program was celebrate "little wins." Every Friday, everyone would post their "little win" for the week. It was amazing to see each person's progress over time, marked by these mini-milestones.

Celebrating small wins makes a huge difference in the momentum you build in your efforts to reach a goal. If you are struggling to find wins you consider worth celebrating, focus on those accomplishments for which you are most grateful.

Gratitude is one most powerful emotional change agents at your disposal. Authentic gratitude not only is born from attitudes of humility and appreciation but reinforces those virtuous attitudes. Gratitude is a natural, positive connector; like gravity, it pulls people together. When you demonstrate and sincerely express gratitude to those who have contributed to even a small achievement, you inspire only greater joy and reciprocal gratitude.

Your brain craves rewards. In response to every instance of positive feedback, the reward center of your brain lights up. Over time, your brain begins to associate certain activities with such rewards, making you *want* to do things because, consciously or sub-consciously, your brain *expects* to be rewarded for doing them. In a nutshell, this is how habits are formed.

"Gratitude is one of the most powerful emotional change agents at your disposal."

Big victories don't happen all at once; rather, they are the culmi-nation of the completion of many smaller milestones. If you wait to celebrate the big victories, completing each of these milestones will be far more difficult and psychologically draining. Expressing grati-tude and celebrating little wins puts gas back in your psychological tank, so to speak, keeping you motivated to consistently do more.

The specific benefits of celebrating small wins are:

• Better awareness of the status of your project;

- A life filled with more conscious awareness of the meaning-fulness, high value, and clear purpose you are experiencing in connection with your efforts (i.e., greater existential fulfillment), which leads to...

- Greater happiness (a wonderful side-effect of greater existential fulfillment); and

- More energy arising from feeling more motivated by the increased activity in the reward center of your brain.

Four Tips for Celebrating Little Wins

Go Small! Obviously, you're celebrating *little wins*, not big ones. So, make sure you've "chunked down" your tasks into tasks with shorter completion intervals. Define clear milestones, and decide, in advance, how you'll celebrate each one. Having a reward to look forward to and then really letting yourself savor the reward once you've earned it is the key to getting the most out of this practice.

Lower Pressure, Relieve Stress. What if you miss your deadline? Give yourself an extension without punishing yourself. Nurture a flexible and easygoing attitude, because, while deadlines are important, they should be guidelines, not absolute rules.

Winners Love Scoreboards. Think baseball scoreboards, where the score is tracked by inning. You want to see your progress as you go. Don't forget to note how far you've come since you started, and mark your progress along your journey. They're called *milestones* for a reason. Celebrate them, and mark them on your "project map" (i.e., your scoreboard), which can be a bulletin board, kanban board, app, spreadsheet, or some other tool that lets you see your progress at a glance.

Learn to Zoom In and Zoom Out. When I'm talking to others about a project, sometimes I start to feel anxiety or worry around whether or not the project is being completed on time. Sometimes, it feels like, because it's not done, or progress is lagging, other people may doubt my ability to complete it at all. This makes me feel like my competence is being questioned. I get defensive, and I feel all tense and anxious.

Counter-productively, I have even found myself avoiding a task or project, because I have felt so bad and anxious about it not being done. *Why isn't it done*, I ask myself. *Why isn't more work happening to finish it?* Ironically, it's precisely because it's not done, yet, and I am too stressed about finishing it to focus on working on it!

Maybe you've experienced this, too.

I have found that the best way to short-circuit this anxiety trap is by zooming in. Instead of focusing on completing the whole project (or a big milestone), I need to narrow my focus to a smaller part of the project—something that seems doable, *right now*. This is taking the work of "chunking down" to another level, chunking down even further!"

If you hit an anxiety pothole, you need to zoom in, chunk down, and rack up an even smaller win. It's not the size of the win that matters to your brain; it's the frequency and consistency with which you light up the reward center that counts! While the celebration of small wins carries many benefits, it is also important to be mindful of potential drawbacks.

Navigating the Pitfalls of Celebrating Small Wins

While celebrating small wins is essential for momentum and motivation, it's important to be cautious of potential pitfalls. One such pitfall is the risk of becoming complacent. In the warmth of celebrating numerous small victories, there's a danger of losing sight of the bigger picture and bigger goals. It's like enjoying the scenic stops so much that you forget you're on a journey to a specific destination.

Another potential issue is the distraction caused by over-celebration. While acknowledging achievements is crucial, excessively reveling in every small success can lead to a loss of focus and time. It's like taking too many breaks during a hike; you enjoy the moments but progress towards the peak slows down considerably.

Moreover, a constant need for small wins can sometimes create a dependency on external validation. This can lead to a situation where the absence of frequent achievements leads to demotivation and a lack of self-drive. It's crucial to find a balance where small wins are celebrated as part of the process, not the end goal. As with any strategy, the key lies in moderation and being conscious of both its strengths and limitations.

Celebrate ALL Your Wins

One is often discouraged from "patting himself on the back," because some see self-promotion as tacky. Here's the thing, though: no one cares as much about your success as you do. Getting others to champion your work starts with you celebrating your accomplishments.

Plus, if one really is doing meaningful work, that means he's doing things that benefit others—a win for everyone. Such work is always worth celebrating. We all need to hear a bit more good news, rather than the 24-hour news cycle's typical doom and gloom. So, celebrate *all* your wins.

KEY TAKEAWAYS

- Celebrating small wins is crucial in building momentum towards achieving larger goals. These mini-milestones can provide motivation and a sense of progress.
- Gratitude is a powerful emotional change agent that not only stems from attitudes of humility and appreciation but also reinforces these virtuous attitudes. It can inspire greater joy and reciprocal gratitude.
- The brain craves rewards and associates certain activities with rewards, leading to the formation of habits. Celebrating small wins can stimulate the reward center of the brain, promoting motivation and habit formation.
- Celebrating small wins can lead to better awareness of project status, greater existential fulfillment, increased happiness, and more energy from feeling motivated.

ACTION ITEMS

- Break down larger tasks into smaller, manageable tasks with clear milestones. Decide in advance how you'll celebrate each milestone.
- Maintain a flexible and easygoing attitude towards deadlines. If a deadline is missed, give yourself an extension without punishing yourself.
- Keep a "scoreboard" or a visual representation of your progress. Mark milestones and celebrate them as they are achieved.
- Learn to zoom in and focus on smaller parts of a project when feeling anxious or overwhelmed. This can help alleviate stress and keep you moving forward.
- Celebrate all your wins, no matter how small. This can help promote a positive mindset and motivate you to continue working towards your goals.

CHAPTER 32

Lead Again

Get the Lead Out

In this final chapter, let's use a quick recap to build critical momentum to launch you out of these pages and further along your journey to recovering your capacity to lead. We have discussed the various aspects of recovering from a personal loss or professional setback, and regaining one's capacity to lead effectively. We have examined the importance of maintaining an indomitable will, cultivating self-respect, and rebuilding trust in oneself and others.

We have also discussed the ongoing process of personal reinvention, the need for virtuous leadership, and the specific traits that effective leaders must cultivate. In addition, we have addressed the issue of dealing with disruption in a wise and enlightened manner, rebuilding trust in one's own ability to lead, and repairing relationships that may have been damaged as a result of a crisis.

Through the practice of mindfulness, self-discovery, and essentialism, leaders can develop the psychological resilience and conative awareness necessary to navigate even the most difficult of situations.

By taking care of their physical and spiritual health, building strong teams, mastering the art of meeting and time management, and learning the other valuable lessons shared in the preceding chapters, leaders can create the conditions for success and rebuild their reputation and trust in others.

Get Started

For those who may want a short, concise list of recommendations for immediate action, I offer the following suggestions based on everything we've covered in this book:

1. Develop and maintain a growth mindset, which will enable you to face fear and failure with determination and resilience.

2. Engage in mindfulness practices and personal growth activities to shape your perspective and promote psychological resilience.

3. Focus on your conative drive and take action to achieve your goals, which will help you overcome adversity and reclaim a sense of calm.

4. Adopt the mindset of essentialism and prioritize your activities to create the conditions for success.

5. Be open to feedback and reframe failure as a learning opportunity, which will facilitate your personal growth and development as a leader.

6. Take care of your physical and spiritual health, and create a supportive team environment that fosters collaboration and success.

7. Manage your time effectively and prioritize the most important tasks in order to maximize your productivity and minimize stress.

While simply doing these seven things, alone, will not empower you to overcome any setback or reclaim your capacity to lead with confidence and resilience, learning well the lessons in this book will give you a foundation for doing so. Therefore, I strongly recommend keeping this book as a reference, writing notes in the margins, underlining, highlighting, and generally using it as a handbook for your leadership recovery journey.

Leadership Recovery: Marathon, Not Sprint

Recovering your capacity to lead will not happen all at once. There may never come a day when you wake up to discover, like magic, everything is all better, now, and you're 100% the leader you have always wanted to be. That is absolutely okay.

Rather than focusing on achieving some perfect state of ideal leadership, remember Bruce Lee's words about goals being targets, not destinations.

> **"A goal is not always meant to be reached; it often serves simply as something to aim at."**

Remember to believe in your ability to grow and adapt, learn to trust God with all the things you cannot control, and relentlessly pursue, with indomitable will, your dreams and goals. With competence, confidence, and trust, cultivate self-leadership, first—master your inner life, build your character, discipline your mind and body —and then you will be fit to lead again.

CHAPTER 33

APPENDIX I

Further Reading

LEADERS ARE READERS

The journey of leadership is continuous, and the quest for knowledge is never-ending. As Sir Francis Bacon wisely noted, "Some books should be tasted, some devoured, but only a few should be chewed and digested thoroughly." The following is a curated list of books that I believe every leader should explore. Whether you choose to taste, devour, or thoroughly digest them, each offers valuable insights for your leadership journey.

Essentialism: The Disciplined Pursuit of Less, Greg McKeown
Why it's recommended: A cornerstone in understanding the power of focus. It's a book I refer to often and one that I believe belongs in every leader's library.

Deep Work: Rules for Focused Success in a Distracted World, Cal Newport

Why it's recommended: Complements the principles in *Essentialism* by diving into strategies for achieving deep, meaningful work amidst a world of distractions.

How to Speak, How to Listen, Mortimer J. Adler

Why it's recommended: A masterpiece on effective communication. Adler's insights are timeless and applicable in any leadership context.

Radical Responsibility: How to Move Beyond Blame, Fearlessly Live Your Highest Purpose, and Become an Unstoppable Force for Good, Fleet Maull, Ph.D.

Why it's recommended: Offers a refreshing perspective on personal accountability and its impact on leadership. A thoughtful read that resonates deeply.

Thinking, Fast and Slow, Daniel Kahneman

Why it's recommended: Essential for understanding cognitive biases and decision-making processes. Kahneman's work is frequently referenced and universally respected.

Common Sense Economics: What Everyone Should Know About Wealth and Prosperity, Gwartney, Stroup, Lee, Ferrarini, & Calhoun

Why it's recommended: Provides clear, accessible insights into economic principles that are crucial for effective leadership.

Lead Together: The Bold, Brave, and Intentional Path to Scaling Your Business, Brent Lowe, Susan Basterfield, & Travis Marsh

Why it's recommended: A great resource for leaders looking to scale their businesses with intentionality and collaboration.

The 4-Hour Workweek, Timothy Ferriss
Why it's recommended: A modern classic that challenges conventional notions of work, productivity, and lifestyle design.

Zero to One, Peter Thiel
Why it's recommended: An insightful guide for startup leaders, offering unique perspectives on innovation and business growth.

Against Empathy: The Case for Rational Compassion, Paul Bloom
Why it's recommended: Bloom challenges conventional views on empathy, arguing for a more balanced and rational approach to compassion. This book is essential for leaders who seek to understand the complexities of emotional intelligence and its application in decision-making. Bloom's insights encourage a nuanced perspective on how leaders can effectively empathize without being overwhelmed by the emotional burdens of others, leading to more objective and impactful leadership decisions.

How to Structure Your Business for Success (3rd ed.), Noel Bagwell
Why it's recommended: My own work, aimed at providing business leaders with foundational knowledge in business organizational structure, contracts, and intellectual property.

The 7 Habits of Highly Effective People, Stephen R. Covey
Why it's recommended: A seminal work on personal and professional effectiveness, Covey's principles are fundamental for any leader.

Dare to Lead: Brave Work. Tough Conversations. Whole Hearts., Brené Brown

Why it's recommended: Brown's exploration of vulnerability and courage in leadership is both inspiring and transformative.

Remember, this list is just a starting point. Your leadership journey is unique, and you may find additional resources that resonate with your personal and professional growth. Happy reading, and may your journey be ever enriched by the wisdom of others.

CHAPTER 34

APPENDIX II

Psychological Safety

WEAVING THE PSYCHOLOGICAL SAFETY NET

Creating psychological safety is akin to weaving a safety net, where each behavior contributes to a stronger, more supportive environment. This appendix, aligned with Chapter 15, offers a series of behavioral exercises designed to foster psychological safety. Presented in alphabetical order, these exercises are the meshes in your safety net—the more you integrate, the more robust your net becomes.

Abandon Assumptions

"What you see is all there is." Resist the "curse of knowledge" bias. Practice humility and patience in communications, clarifying assumptions and ensuring mutual understanding.

Reflective Question: How can I better clarify my assumptions in conversations today?

Accept Complexity

Recognize the inherent complexity in situations and people. Embrace humility and ask open-ended questions to uncover layers you might have missed.

Real-life Example: Instead of oversimplifying a team member's challenge, ask, "Can you help me understand the complexities of this issue?"

Accept Encouragement

Graciously accept compliments. See them as affirmations of your potential and express sincere gratitude.

Practical Tip: Next time you receive a compliment, pause and internally acknowledge its potential truth before responding with thanks.

Accept Others and Yourself

Embrace the diversity and complexity in others and yourself. Practice mindfulness to encounter and understand different perspectives and inner challenges.

Reflective Question: How can I demonstrate acceptance and appreciation for diversity in my team today?

Actively Listen

Engage in active listening. Open your mind and heart, thoughtfully understand, and consider what others say without rushing to respond.

Application: In your next meeting, repeat back what you've heard to ensure clarity and understanding.

Affirm Dignity

Acknowledge the inherent dignity in every individual as a creation of divine love. Let this recognition guide your interactions.

Practical Tip: In conversations, remind yourself of the intrinsic value of each person you're engaging with.

Attend Somatic Cues

Be attentive to body language in others, responding appropriately to foster safety and respect.

Real-life Example: Notice a team member's closed-off body language during a meeting and check in with them afterward.

Avoid Blaming and Extrapolation

Replace blame with curiosity. View challenges as learning opportunities rather than attributing fault.

Application: When faced with a setback, ask, "What can we learn from this?"

Broaden Your Interests

Show interest in the passions of others. This fosters deeper connections and demonstrates your care.

Real-life Example: Participate in a team hobby or interest, even if it's new to you.

Challenge Yourself

Embrace the discomfort of growth. Acknowledge the effort needed to integrate these practices into your leadership style.

Reflective Question: Which of these practices challenges me the most, and how can I approach it today?

Eliminate Distractions

Ensure full presence in interactions. This cultivates deeper connections and shows respect.

Practical Tip: In your next conversation, put away digital devices and give undivided attention.

Embrace Uncertainty

Accept and find peace in the uncertain aspects of life. This fosters resilience and adaptability.

Reflective Question: How can I demonstrate openness to uncertainty in my leadership today?

Forgive and Make Amends

Practice forgiveness and making amends. This builds trust and repairs relationships.

Application: Reflect on any unresolved conflicts and take steps towards reconciliation.

Hold Space

Provide a non-judgmental space for others to express themselves. This nurtures trust and openness.

Real-life Example: In a team discussion, encourage open sharing without immediately offering solutions.

Memento Mori

Reflect on the impermanence of life to gain perspective on current challenges and priorities.

Reflective Exercise: Spend a few moments each day contemplating the finite nature of life and how it influences your priorities.

Nurture Others and Yourself

Focus on caring for others and self-care. This ensures sustainability and effectiveness in your leadership.

Practical Tip: Schedule daily self-care activities and actively look for ways to support your team's well-being.

Practice Acceptance, Optimism, and Receptivity

Accept difficult situations, maintain a practical optimistic outlook, and be receptive to others' contributions.

Application: When facing challenges, focus on what can be learned and improved.

Practice Sympathy and Vulnerability

Show genuine concern and vulnerability. This deepens connections and fosters a supportive environment.

Reflective Question: How can I show vulnerability in a way that strengthens my team's trust in my leadership?

Prioritize Service and Pursue Equanimity

Serve others selflessly and seek inner calm
and balance in your leadership approach.

Application: Regularly assess how your actions serve the greater good of your team and community.

Recognize and Stop Overthinking

Identify patterns of overthinking and replace them with constructive habits like meditation or problem-solving.

Practical Tip: When you catch yourself overthinking, pause and engage in a brief mindfulness exercise.

Suspend Judgment and Thoughtfully Question

Practice withholding judgment until fully informed. Ask insightful questions to deepen understanding.

Application: In discussions, focus on gathering information before forming conclusions.

Volunteer First

Take initiative in leadership opportunities. This demonstrates ambition and a commitment to growth.

Application: Look for opportunities in your organization where you can lead a new project or initiative.

By integrating these practices into your leadership, you weave a robust psychological safety net, fostering an environment of trust, respect, and growth. This list is not exhaustive; feel free to add practices that resonate with your unique leadership style and organizational culture.

About the Author

Meet Noel Bagwell

Noel R. Bagwell, III is a distinguished attorney, author, speaker, and transformative leadership coach rooted in Nashville, Tennessee.

As the visionary founder of Counsel & Clarity™, Noel has dedicated his career to fostering growth and resilience in both businesses and individuals. With over a decade of legal expertise, he is renowned for his preventive legal strategies aimed at growth-stage companies, reducing risk and promoting enterprise success beyond traditional billable hours.

Noel's influence extends beyond his written work and coaching, as he is a sought-after public speaker with over 5,000 event attendees, enriching lives through workshops, seminars, and Continuing Legal Education courses. His contributions have earned him numerous accolades, including the TN Supreme Court's Attorney for Justice award five times and the Clarksville TN Mayor's Certificate for servant leadership.

Living near Nashville, TN, with his son, Liam, Noel's life is filled with joy, curiosity, and a profound commitment to making a difference. His work not only aims to save his clients millions but also focuses on crafting transformative experiences that lead to growth and resilience.

Connect with Noel

Web: https://counselandclarity.com/
E-mail: contact@counselandclarity.com

REFERENCES

[1] Argyris, C. (1991). Teaching smart people how to learn. Harvard Business Review, 69(3), 99-109.

[2] Greenleaf, R. K. (1977). Servant Leadership: A Journey into the Nature of Legitimate Power and Greatness. Paulist Press.

[3] Chernow, R. (2010). Washington: A Life. Penguin Press.

[4] Hackman, M. Z., & Johnson, C. E. (2009). Leadership: A communication perspective. Waveland Press. / Bass, B. M., & Riggio, R. E. (2006). Transformational leadership (2nd ed.). Psychology Press.

[5] Philippians 4:11-12 (RSVCE).

[6] Various Users. What is the meaning of the zen quote: "before Enlightenment Chop Wood, carry water. after Enlightenment Chop Wood, carry water"? Buddhism Stack Exchange. Retrieved November 4, 2022, from https://buddhism.stackexchange.com/questions/15921/what-is-the-meaning-of-the-zen-quote-before-enlightenment-chop-wood-carry-wat

[7] Kahneman, D. (2011). *Thinking, Fast and Slow*. Farrar, Straus and Giroux.

[8] NeuroTray. (n.d.). How many bits of information can the brain process? NeuroTray. Retrieved from https://neurotray.com/how-many-bits-of-information-can-the-brain-process/

[9] Proverbs 24:30–31.

[10] (Kahneman, D. 2011).

[11] Boogaard, K. (2022, February 17). How To Write Smart Goals (With Examples). Work Life by Atlassian. Retrieved October 18, 2022, from https://www.atlassian.com/blog/productivity/how-to-write-smart-goals

[12] Proverbs 9:8.

[13] Proverbs 12:15.

[14] Catechism of the Catholic Church (2nd ed.): 1766. Cf. St Thomas Aquinas, Sth I-II, 26, *corp. art.*; St. Augustine, *De Trin.*, 8,3,4:PL 42,949-950; and St. Augustine, *De Civ. Dei* 14, 7, 2:PL 41,410.

[15] Sirach 37:11.

[16] Norman, E. (2022, June 30). Trust in government lower now than after Watergate scandal. RealClearPolitics.com. Retrieved September 6, 2022, from https://www.realclearpolitics.com/articles/2022/06/30/trust_in_government_lower_now_than_after_watergate_scandal_147819.html

[17] Roberts, N. F. (2020, September 1). The psychology of trust explains how institutions can regain it once lost. Forbes. Retrieved September 5, 2022, from https://www.forbes.com/sites/nicolefisher/2020/09/01/the-psychology-of-trust--how-institutions-can-regain-it-once-lost/

[18] Romans 12:16-18, 21

[19] 1 Corinthians 13

[20] Hauk, C. (2021). Shine: Ignite Your Inner Game to Lead Consciously at Work and in the World (1st edition). Sounds True.

[21] Bottaro, G. (2018) The Mindful Catholic: Finding God One Moment at a Time (p. 15). Wellspring. Kindle Edition.

[22] *Id.*

[23] Mark 7:20-22 (RSVCE).

[24] Luke 6:45 (RSVCE).

[25] Bunkley, Nick (March 3, 2008). "Joseph Juran, 103, Pioneer in Quality Control, Dies". The New York Times.

[26] McKeown, G. (2014). Chapter 3: Discern: The Unimportance of Practically Everything. In *Essentialism: The Disciplined Pursuit of Less*. Crown Business.

[27] Bunkley, Nick (March 3, 2008). "Joseph Juran, 103, Pioneer in Quality Control, Dies". The New York Times.

[28] McKeown, G. (2014). Chapter 3: Discern: The Unimportance of Practically Everything. In *Essentialism: The Disciplined Pursuit of Less*. Crown Business. Citing John Maxwell, Developing the Leader Within You (Nashville, TN: T. Nelson, 1993), 22–23.

[29] Sowell, T. (2007). *A Conflict of Visions: Ideological Origins of Political Struggles*. Basic Books.

[30] Lisefski, B. (2021, September 9). The Big Lie of "Good, Fast, Cheap". Medium. Retrieved September 4, 2022, from https://medium.com/swlh/the-big-lie-of-good-fast-cheap-fb8905818250

[31] Foxworthy, E. (2022, April 13). What about weight discrimination? National Institutes of Health. Retrieved November 14, 2022, from https://www.edi.nih.gov/blog/communities/what-about-weight-discrimination

[32] *Id.*

[33] Eidelson, J. (2022, March 15). *Weight Discrimination Remains Legal In Most of the U.S.* Bloomberg.com. Retrieved November 14, 2022, from https://www.bloomberg.com/news/features/2022-03-15/weight-discrimination-remains-legal-in-most-of-the-u-s

[34] *Id.*

[35] *Id.*

[36] Bloom, P. (2018). *Against Empathy: The Case for Rational Compassion* (Reprint Edition). Ecco.

[37] American Academy of Neurology. (2019, January 30). Exercise may improve thinking skills in people as young as 20. *ScienceDaily*. Retrieved November 13, 2022 from www.sciencedaily.com/releases/2019/01/190130161638.htm

[38] Centers for Disease Control and Prevention. (2021). Healthy Weight, Nutrition, and Physical Activity. https://www.cdc.gov/healthyweight/index.html

[39] *Id.*

[40] Valdes, A. M., Walter, J., Segal, E., & Spector, T. D. (2018). Role of the gut microbiota in nutrition and health. BMJ, 361, k2179. https://www.bmj.com/content/361/bmj.k2179

[41] *Id.*

[42] *Id.*

[43] (CDC, 2021)

[44] Hoffer, E. (1951). *The True Believer*. Harper & Row.

[45] *Id.*

[46] Moffitt, P. (2021, January 25). *The Tyranny of Expectations*. Dharma Wisdom. Retrieved November 14, 2022, from https://dharmawisdom.org/the-tyranny-of-expectations/

[47] Fairchild, M. (2020, October 28). *The sin of pride according to the Bible*. Learn Religions. Retrieved November 14, 2022, from https://www.learnreligions.com/the-sin-of-pride-according-to-the-bible-5080290

[48] Catechism of the Catholic Church 2559. Cf. CCC 2613.

[49] Menezes, F. W. (2016, January 1). Mercy is who god is. it's Love's second name. The Fathers of Mercy. Retrieved February 18, 2023, from https://fathersofmercy.com/extraordinary-jubilee-year-of-mercy-jubilee-year-of-mercy-mercy-fathers-of-mercy-mercy-minute-fr-wade-menezes/

[50] Matthew 6:14-15 (RSVCE).

[51] CCC 1808.

[52] Wisdom 8:2 (RSCVCE)

[53] What Makes a Great Executive Retreat - Harvard Business Review. https://hbr.org/2022/07/what-makes-a-great-executive-retreat.

[54] 27 Best Team Retreat Ideas You'll Ever Need - Science of People. https://www.scienceofpeople.com/team-retreat-ideas/.

[55] Economy, P. (2019, January 11). *A new study of 19 million meetings reveals that meetings waste more* ... Inc.com. Retrieved November 24, 2022, from https://www.inc.com/peter-economy/a-new-study-of-19000000-meetings-reveals-that-meetings-waste-more-time-than-ever-but-there-is-a-solution.html

[56] Rosenstein, J. (2013, March 25). The Five Secrets To Leading Great Meetings. HuffPost. Retrieved November 30, 2023, from https://www.huffpost.com/entry/the-five-secrets-to-leadi_b_2951339.

[57] (McKeown, 2014).